MĀYĀ IN RADHAKRISHNAN'S THOUGHT

MĀYĀ
IN
RADHAKRISHNAN'S THOUGHT
SIX MEANINGS OTHER THAN ILLUSION

DONALD A. BRAUE

South Asia Books

SOUTH ASIA BOOKS
Box 502, Columbia, Missouri, 65205

First Edition : 1985

ISBN: 0-8364-1129-3

Printed in India by Shantilal Jain at Shri Jainendra Press, A-45, Phase I, Naraina, New Delhi 110 028 and published by Narendra Prakash Jain, for Motilal Banarsidass, Delhi 110 007.

To

DAVID CHARLES BRAUE

my only son,

that he and his generation might strive for a balance of scientific knowledge and the knowledge of God.

Foreword

Gradually, but only very gradually, the horizons of contemporary western philosophy are broadening to include the philosophies of the great Asian civilizations. The reasons for the parochialism of western philosophy are many, and need not be recited again here. Let us rejoice that we are beginning to have the wider view that the very concept of philosophy demands and deserves.

In this widening of horizons, Donald Braue's essay on Sarvepalli Radhakrishnan's interpretation of *māyā* can play a very useful part, for it constitutes excellent analysis of a key concept in the work of a great contemporary philosopher.

It is fashionable in some circles in both India and the west to speak condescendingly of Radhakrishnan. I venture to predict that Radhakrishnan's work will long outlast these present detractors. True, the work of any pioneer can be extended, corrected, emended. But there must be pioneers, and surely Radhakrishnan was one. His work is well worth the analysis Braue here performs.

But *six* meanings for *māyā* ? Let the reader come to his own conclusion on this matter as he makes his way through Braue's pages, and then turns to the appendix for Radhakrishnan's own words. Yet if there are six meanings, some readers will come directly to the conclusion that here is an example of the egregious ambiguity which muddies the waters of philosophical discourse.

Let me attempt in a brief paragraph to meet this issue head-on. Cognitive meaning, I wish to argue, is in most significant instances constituted by two components or aspects. Let us call them the *formal* and the *contextual* aspects of meaning. So for example in most common nouns the formal element predominates. This is the dictionary meaning of a word. Yet even here most good dictionaries append examples of the use of the word being defined, thereby calling attention to a contextual aspect or component of meaning. This contextual element becomes virtually total in proper nouns. It is obviously present in pronouns, especially demonstrative pronouns such as "this" and "that".

I bring up these linguistic details only in order to argue that in Radhakrishnan's interpretation of *māyā* (and in other interpretations too) we have a notable instance of a basic philosophic term in which a significant portion of the meaning has to be dug out of context.

It remains only to add that this aspect of Radhakrishnan's philosophy holds true also for the basic terms of other philosophers and philosophies. Let the reader supply his own examples.

John A. Hutchison
Claremont, California

Preface

Is it the case that an attitude of world-negation characterizes the majority of people in India? Is such an attitude preached by the Upaniṣads or the *Bhagavadgītā*? The alleged attitude of world-negation in India has been associated with the symbol *māyā*. This verbal symbol has been linked to a belief in the unreality of the world. I became interested in studying whether the doctrine of *māyā* as popularly understood was a necessary part of Hindu belief and this book emerged as the result.

My academic training through college and seminary took me deep into the river of western philosophy and Christian theology. However, most of my otherwise excellent teachers felt deeply that the classical traditions of eastern civilizations were not worthy of any serious consideration. Not until I entered graduate school did I have the opportunity to study with a philosopher of religion who knew both the western tradition and the classical texts of India. I am pleased and proud that he wrote the Foreword for this book.

While studying under John Hutchison I looked through the writings of Sir Sarvepalli Radhakrishnan. I sensed immediately a profound preoccupation with cross-cultural philosophy of religion in them. Here was a magnificent, prolific Hindu writer who challenged my own Christian faith in a constructive, illuminating way. My marginal notations in his books are not all complimentary. But in Radhakrishnan's writings I found an engaging, fruitful entry into the heart and mind of India.

Keeping the focus of my attention on a single idea in Radhakrishnan's thought was difficult. His exposition of ideas is many-sided, not sequential. It illustrates his way of thinking so characteristic of India's intellectual giants and so inimical to an Aristotelian approach. Radhakrishnan weaves the thread of *māyā* into a colorful fabric composed of many interesting ideas. I was often tempted to follow other threads than the one which constitutes the meaning of *māyā*.

I gratefully acknowledge help from many persons. Fine editorial suggestions came from Dr. N. Gerald Barrier, Professor of History at the University of Missouri and Managing Proprietor of South Asia Books. Leah Flowers typed the final manuscript with great care. Three persons at Texas Christian University provided financial help: Dr. Larry Adams, Associate Vice Chancellor for Graduate Studies and Research; Dr. Michael McCracken, Dean, AddRan College of Arts and Sciences; and Dr. Kenneth Lawrence, Chairperson, Department of Religion-Studies. Marcia Braue kindly drew the pencil portrait of President Radhakrishnan which appears as the frontispiece. Judith Oelfke Smith designed the cover with her usual mastery of symbolic meaning and artistic line.

Many teachers have influenced me positively through their examples of tireless dedication and painstaking research. Students have also helped through the inquisitiveness in their eyes as I lectured about this or that aspect of Asian thought. Though they are too numerous to mention individually, my gratitude is nonetheless heartfelt.

I wish to thank Dr. and Mrs. Vishwanath S. Naravané for their hospitality at Shanti Niwas, Allahabad and for our pleasant contacts in America. I also thank Partha and Jhumur Ghosh of New Delhi for their kindness. It symbolizes the deep, friendly relations that are possible between the peoples of the two largest democracies in the world.

Donald A. Braue
Sparta, New Jersey

Contents

Abbreviations

[*The date in parenthesis is the original publication date.*]

BG	*The Bhagavadgitā* (1948)
BS	*The Brahma Sūtra : The Philosophy of Spiritual Life* (1960)
CL	*The Creative Life* (1975)
D	*The Dhammapada* (1950)
ERWT	*Eastern Religions and Western Thought* (1939)
EW	*East and West : Some Reflections* (1956)
EWR	*East and West in Religion* (1933)
FC	*Freedom and Culture* (1936)
FS	*Fellowship of the Spirit* (1961)
HH	*The Heart of Hindusthan* (1936)
HPEW, I	*History of Philosophy, Eastern and Western,* volume one (1952)
HVL	*The Hindu View of Life* (1926)
IC	*India and China* (1944)
IP, I	*Indian Philosophy,* volume one (1923)
IP, II	*Indian Philosophy,* volume two (1927)
IR	*Indian Religions* (1979)
IVL	*An Idealist View of Life* (1932)
Kalki	*Kalki—or the Future of Civilization* (1929)
MG	*Mahatma Gandhi : Essays and Reflections on his Life and Work* (1939)
OH	*Our Heritage* (1973)
OSW, 1952-1959	*Occasional Speeches and Writings, October* 1952-*February* 1959 (1960)
PCF	*The Present Crisis of Faith* (1970)
PRSW, Second Series	*President Radhakrishnan's Speeches and Writings, Second Series, May* 1964-*May* 1967 (1969)
PRT	*The Philosophy of Rabindranath Tagore* (1918)

PU	*The Principal Upaniṣads* (1953)
RC	*Religion and Culture* (1968)
RCW	*Religion in a Changing World* (1967)
RF	*Recovery of Faith* (1956)
RRCP	*The Reign of Religion in Contemporary Philosophy* (1920)
RS	*Religion and Society* (1947)
RWN	*The Religion We Need* (1928)
WUS	*The World's Unborn Soul* (1936)

1

Introduction

I. Sarvepalli Radhakrishnan : A Biographical Sketch

For a complete, critical biography of Sarvepalli Radhakrishnan,[1] our primary sources are unfortunately meager since he refused politely but persistently to write a full autobiography[2]. The following sketch merely highlights a few facts[3] which would form the skeleton of a full-fledged biography.

1. See "Chronology," in Radhakrishnan: *Selected Writings on Philosophy, Religion, and Culture*, ed. Robert A. McDermott (New York: E. P. Dutton and Company, Inc., 1970; a Dutton Paperback), pp. 27-28; S. J. Samartha, *Introduction to Radhakrishnan*: *The Man and His Thought* (New York: Association Press, 1964), pp. 14-19; Thomas Paul Urumpackal, *Organized Religion According to Dr. S. Radhakrishnan* (Rome: Universita Gregoriana Editrice, 1972), pp. 6-13; Ishwar C. Harris, "The Concept of Universalism in the Philosophy of Sarvepalli Radhakrishnan" (Ph.D. dissertation, Claremont Graduate School, 1974), pp. 159-160. Radhakrishnan's movements during the period 1952-1967 are documented in the footnotes to his occasional speeches and writings which have been published by The Director, Publications Division, Ministry of Information and Broadcasting, Government of India, Patiala House, New Delhi 1.

2. "My Search for Truth" an essay published in *Religion in Transition*, ed. Vergilius Ferm (London: George Allen and Unwin, 1937), pp. 11-59; reprinted in *Radhakrishnan*: *Selected Writings on Philosophy, Religion, and Culture*, ed. Robert A. McDermott (New York: E. P. Dutton and Company, Inc., 1970), pp. 35-65 (hereafter cited as McDermott, ed., *Radhakrishnan*). There are also some auto-biographical details in "The Religion of the Spirit and the World's Need: Fragments of a Confession" (hereafter cited as "Confession"), in *The Philosophy of Sarvepalli Radhakrishnan*, ed. Paul Arthur Schilpp (New York: Tudor Publishing Company, 1952), pp. 5-82.

3. Anna Rothe and Evelyn Lohr, eds. *Current Biography*: *Who's News and*

Radhakrishnan's reluctance to write about himself is seen in his reply to Paul Arthur Schilpp's request for more autobiographical details : "I am not persuaded that the events of my life are of much interest to the readers of this volume."[4] This sentiment is in keeping with the South Asian tradition. Indian intellectuals down through the centuries have tended to look beyond historical dates and places in order to focus on transcendental ideals. In no small measure this may be due to interpretations of *māyā* which have tended to minimize the significance of historical particularity. More fundamentally, the tendency to avoid autobiographical details is consistent with the traditional Indian view of history in which life repeats itself without end. Even though Radhakrishnan's brief autobiography is rich with insights into the inner events of his life, it is destitute of details regarding outer events. His reluctance to write about himself is documented by the fact that he describes the first twenty years of his life in four sentences:

> I spent the first eight years of my life (1888-1896) in a small town in South India, Tirutani, which is even today a great centre of religious pilgrimage. My parents were religious in the traditional sense of the term. I studied in Christian Missionary institutions for twelve years, Lutheran Mission High School, Tirupati (1896-1900), Voorhees' College, Vellore (1900-1904), and the Madras Christian College (1904-1908). Thus I grew up in an atmosphere where the unseen was a living reality.[5]

In addition to biographical facts, the reader's attention is invited

---

Why, 1952 (New York: The H. W. Wilson Company, 1953), pp. 487-490. *The International Who's Who*, 1974-1975, 28th ed. (London: Europa Publications Ltd., 1974), p. 1415; *Who's Who*, 1974-1975: *An Annual Biographical Dictionary* (New York: St. Martin's Press, 1974), pp. 2682-2683; and Clare D. Kinsman, ed., *Contemporary Authors—Permanent Series: A Bio-Bibliographical Guide to Current Authors and Their Works*, vol. 1 (Detroit, Michigan: Gale Research Company, 1975), p. 526. "Radhakrishnan of India, Philosopher, Dead at 86," Obituary in *The New York Times* 124 (17 April 1975): 42. Obituaries on Radhakrishnan in *Time* 105 (28 April 1975): 82 and in *Newsweek* 85 (28 April 1975): 63.

4. This letter is reproduced in facsimile at the beginning of his "Confession," in Schilpp, ed.

5. "Confession," in Schilpp, ed., p. 6.

to Radhakrishnan's confession regarding "the unseen as a living reality." This theme with many variations will recur throughout our study of his writings.

Sarvepalli Radhakrishnan was the son of Sarvepalli Veeraswami and Seethamma, Telugu Brahmins. His brief autobiographical essay begins :

> I was born on September 5, 1888, at a small place, Tirutani, forty miles to the north-west of Madras, in South India, the second child of Hindu parents, who were conventional in their religious outlook. I have not had any advantages of birth or of wealth. The early years of my life till twelve were spent in Tirutani and Tirupati, both famous as pilgrim centres. I cannot account for the fact that from the time I knew myself I have had firm faith in the reality of an unseen world behind the flux of phenomena, a world which we apprehend not with the senses but with the mind, and even when I was faced by grave difficulties, this faith has remained unshaken.[6]

His attitude of conviction regarding "the reality of an unseen world behind the flux of phenomena" is a noteworthy variation on the recurring theme mentioned above.

Radhakrishnan's education in Christian missionary institutions stirred him to examine his own Hindu tradition with vigor and deep resolve. Regarding his years at a Lutheran High School in Tirupati, Voorhees College, and Madras Christian College, Radhakrishnan recalls : "My pride as a Hindu roused by the enterprise and eloquence of Swami Vivekananda was deeply hurt by the treatment accorded to Hinduism in missionary institutions."[7] But instead of rejecting outright what his teachers said, even when it cut him to the core, Radhakrishnan set out to discover what was valuable in his own religious tradition and in the religious traditions of others. This enterprise seems to have continued throughout his entire career and no intellectual in our time has done more than he to interpret Eastern philosophy and religion to the Western world.

In 1905 while at Voorhees College Radhakrishnan married

6. "My Search for Truth," in McDermott, ed., *Radhakrishnan*, p. 35.
7. "My Search for Truth," in McDermott, ed., *Radhakrishnan*, p. 37.

Sivakamamma.[8] They had been married more than fifty years when she died in 1956. They had five daughters and one son. Their son and youngest child, Sarvepalli Gopal, was born 23 April 1923.[9] A historian and biographer, Dr. Gopal is the author of numerous books on contemporary history in South Asia and the general editor of *Selected Works of Jawaharlal Nehru.* Gopal became a Fellow of St. Anthony's College, Oxford in 1966 and has also been Commonwealth Fellow at Trinity College, Cambridge. He was appointed Professor of Contemporary History at Jawaharlal Nehru University, New Delhi in 1972. He has served his country in many ways, including as Chairman of the National Book Trust, India (1973-1976).

Sarvepalli Radhakrishnan's professional career had three phases which overlapped: teacher of philosophy, leader in higher education, and statesman. His career as teacher of philosophy spanned the years from 1909 to 1952. He received the M.A. degree in philosophy from Madras Christian College in 1909. Principal Hobbs of Madras Presidency College saw the promise in Radhakrishnan's work and appointed him as a lecturer for the Provincial Education Service at one hundred rupees a month. In 1911 Radhakrishnan was appointed assistant professor of philosophy at Madras Presidency College. In 1916 he was advanced to full professor. In 1917 he was transferred to the Arts College at Rajahmundry (Madras) as a lecturer in philosophy. From 1918 to 1921 he was University Professor of Philosophy at the new University of Mysore. During these three years he completed *The Philosophy of Rabindranath Tagore* (1918) and *The Reign of Religion in Contemporary Philosophy* (1920). The latter made him well known in the philosophical world. Sir Ashutosh Mukherjee, the then Vice Chancellor of the University of Calcutta, was among those who noticed the emerging scholar. He offered Radhakrishnan the King George V Chair of Mental and Moral Science, a chair which Radhakrishnan was to occupy from 1921 to 1931 and again from 1937 to 1941. Radhakrishnan himself describes the King George V Chair as "the most important

8. Another source says he married Sivakamamma in May, 1903.

9. Facts about S. Gopal have been gleaned from *Who's Who* 1981-1982 (New York: St. Martin's Press, 1981), p. 1009 and *The Writers Directory* 1982-1984 (Detroit, Michigan: Gale Research Company, 1981), p. 351.

philosophy chair in India."[10] The manuscript for volume one of *Indian Philosophy* was sent to the publisher in December, 1921 and the book appeared in 1923. Volume two of this contribution to the Muirhead Library of Philosophy appeared in 1927. *Indian Philosophy* seems to have launched Radhakrishnan's professional career into global orbit. In 1926 the Indian professor of philosophy was off to Oxford, England. He narrates :

> Through my articles in the *Hibbert Journal*, I was brought into contact with its editor, Dr. L. P. Jacks, late Principal of Manchester College, Oxford, who graciously invited me to give the Upton Lectures on *The Hindu View of Life*, in 1926, in his college. I was enabled to accept his invitation, as the University of Calcutta deputed me to represent it at the Congress of the Universities of the British Empire in June, 1926, and the International Congress of Philosophy at the Harvard University in September, 1926.[11]

That the interpretation of *māyā* was of concern to Radhakrishnan is documented by the fact that at this international meeting of philosophers in Cambridge, Massachusetts he presented a paper entitled "The Doctrine of Māyā: Some Problems." While in the United States he delivered the Haskell Lectures in Comparative Religion at the University of Chicago. Meanwhile back in India, Radhakrishnan served as Chairperson of the Executive Council, Indian Philosophical Congress (1925-1937) and General President of the Third Session of that Congress in Bombay (1927). He also served as President of the Post-Graduate Council in Arts (1927-1931). In 1929 Radhakrishnan was invited to deliver the Hibbert Lectures at the Universities of London and Manchester. They appeared as *An Idealist View of Life*. While in England he delivered a second series of Upton Lectures at Oxford. In 1931 the Indian professor of philosophy was knighted by King George V. After a five-year administrative interlude as Vice-Chancellor of Andhra University, Waltair, Sir Sarvepalli's teaching career took him back to Oxford University where in 1936 he was appointed to the Spalding Chair of Eastern Reli-

10. "My search for Truth," in McDermott, ed. *Radhakrishnan*, pp. 43-44.
11. Ibid., pp. 44-45.

gions and Ethics. He occupied simultaneously the Spalding Chair at Oxford and the King George V Chair at Calcutta. His lectures at Oxford during 1936-1938 constitute *Eastern Religions and Western Thought.* The outbreak of World War II in 1939 forced him to give up his annual voyages to England. In 1939 he took a top administrative post at Benares Hindu University in Varanasi (Benares). In 1941 he resigned from the King George V Chair in philosophy at Calcutta University in order to accept the Sir Sayaji Rao Gaekwad Chair in Indian Culture and Civilization at Benares Hindu University. He continued to occupy the Spalding Chair in England until 1952 when he became Professor Emeritus at Oxford.

The second phase of Radhakrishnan's professional career was his leadership in higher education. His career as university administrator spanned the years from 1931 to 1962. In 1931 he became Vice Chancellor of Andhra University in Waltair, a post he held until 1936. Simultaneously he served as a member of the International Committee on Intellectual Cooperation of the League of Nations (1931-1939). During this period Radhakrishnan delivered convocation addresses at universities all over India. Some of these addresses to university audiences are collected in an important but rare book, *Freedom and Culture* (1936). In that same year, some of his journal articles written during the early 1920's were collected and published again as *The Heart of Hindusthan.* After the interlude of lecturing at Oxford, Radhakrishnan's career as university administrator resumed with his appointment as Vice Chancellor, Benares Hindu University, Varanasi (1939-1948). During World War II he delivered the prestigious Kamala Lectures at the Universities of Calcutta and Benares (1942). These lectures during a time of global upheaval focused on the need for social reconstruction in the light of religious ideals. They appeared as *Religion and Society* (1947) and in today's world it deserves more attention than what is usually given to Radhakrishnan's scholarship. During World War II he also lectured at universities in China. Appearing as *India and China* (1944), these lectures deal with Confucianism, Taoism, and Chinese Buddhism. More convocation addresses and other speeches delivered between 1937 and 1944 were published by the International Book Service in Poona as *Education, Politics, and War* (1944).[12] After World War II Radhakrishnan headed the Indian delegation to UNESCO (1946-1950). He arrived in New York aboard the Queen Mary on 18 March 1946 for the first session of UNESCO. Supported by the Watumull Foundation, Radhakriṣhnan went on a month-long United States lecture tour which included fourteen universities and assorted learned societies.[13] In 1947 he led the Indian delegation to the UNESCO Conference in Mexico City. He was a member of the Executive Board of UNESCO (1946-1951), its chairperson in 1948-1949, and president of UNESCO's seventh general conference in 1952. His contributions to the League of Nations and the United Nations show that his educational leadership was felt in the international arena. Yet he continued to provide educational leadership at home. Radhakrishnan chaired the University Commission of the Government of India from 1948 to 1949. He was president of the Indian PEN organization from 1949 and vice-president of International PEN from 1956. PEN is an organization for poets, playwrights, editors, essayists, and novelists. Even after Radhakrishnan entered the statesman phase of his professional career he continued to provide leadership in higher education. He was Chancellor of Delhi University from 1953 to 1962.

Radhakrishnan's career as statesman began about 1947 when The Republic of India emerged from more than two hundred years of British rule. He was a member of the Indian Constituent Assembly (1947-1949) which drafted the present Constitution of India. With the Mahātma and others he helped formulate the system of government of the largest democracy in the world. In 1949 Jawaharlal Nehru named him India's first Ambassador to the Soviet Union. The "Preface" to Radhakrishnan's translation of *The Principal Upaniṣads* (1953) was written in the embassy. On 18 April 1952 Radhakrishnan resigned his embassy post in Moscow at Nehru's request in order to become the Congress Party's candidate for Vice-President of

12. This bibliography of Radhakrishnan's publications presented in chronological order was compiled, with Radhakrishnan's help, by T. R. V. Murti. It appears as "Writings of Sarvepalli Radhakrishnan to March, 1952," in Schilpp, ed., pp. 846-861. It has been indispensable for this research project.

13. *Newsweek* 27 (1 April 1946) : 89.

India. As Vice-President of The Republic of India for two consecutive five-year terms (1952-1962), Radhakrishnan presided over the Rajya Sabha or Upper House of Parliament in New Delhi. He was in constant demand as a speaker and lecturer but his quiet scholarly activity continued. For instance, Vice-President Radhakrishnan published a book which may emerge as one of his most important long-term scholarly contributions, his introduction to, translation of, and notes on *The Brahma Sūtra* (1960). In 1962, Radhakrishnan was elected to a five-year term as President of The Republic of India. These were critical years surrounding the death of Prime Minister Jawaharlal Nehru. Sir Sarvepalli had taught Nehru's daughter, Indira Gandhi, at Oxford in the 1930's. So as President, the philosopher and statesman spanned two generations of politicians, a symbol of stability in changing times. His many speeches and writings during fifteen years in high public office have been published by the Government of India in a series of thick volumes.[14] In May, 1967 the seventy-eight year old statesman retired from the Presidency and left New Delhi. His retirement years were spent at "Girija"[15] in Madras. Since 1968, four Orient Paperbacks containing selections from his earlier writings have been distributed by Hind Pocket Books, Limited: *Religion and Culture* (1968), *The Present Crisis of Faith* (1970), *Our Heritage* (1973), and *The Creative Life* (1975). A similar Vision Books paperback has also appeared, *Indian Religions* (1979). The lasting appeal of these books is testimony to the ability of this philosophy professor, chancellor, and statesman to communicate with people in all walks of life.

Sir Sarvepalli Radhakrishnan died of heart failure in a Madras nursing home on 17 April 1975 after a prolonged illness. He was cremated the same day with full state honors. After elaborate Hindu rites, his son, Dr. Sarvepalli Gopal, lighted the funeral pyre. Radhakrishnan was a vegetarian, non-smoker, and teetotaler. Reading was his favorite leisure activity. He enjoyed cricket, often joining his grandchildren in a game. His memberships, awards, and honors would make a very long list and he would probably be the first one to pass over such a list, anyway.

14. They can be obtained from The Director of The Publications Division, Government of India, New Delhi.

15. "Girija" is a lovely mansion at 30 Edward Eliots Road, Madras, India.

He received honorary degrees from the University of London, Oxford University, Cambridge University, and more than fifty other universities. A famous teacher of philosophy, educational leader, and statesman is dead. But an equally famous scholar is alive and well both in his writings which continue to attract well-deserved attention and in his speeches which echo in the memories of those fortunate enough to have heard him speak.

II. The Problem of Māyā

There would be no problem of *māyā* if there were no impetus to understand the axiological and soteriological status of the world. But, as Radhakrishnan contends, "search for a philosophical view is a necessity of our nature."[16] Elsewhere he posits "a metaphysical curiosity for a theoretical explanation of the world."[17] In an address to the Vishwa Hindu Dharma Sammelan in New Delhi, 10 December 1965 he claimed :

> Every human individual has the craving to find out what this world consists of. Is this cosmic panorama all ? Or is there a constant presence behind, informing, animating and giving life to this whole cosmic process ? It is the question which we raise. Every thoughtful person has raised it.[18]

Radhakrishnan's affirmation of a "constant presence" behind the cosmic panorama is another variation on the theme already noted—Radhakrishnan's firm faith in the reality of an unseen world behind the flux of phenomena.

The problem of *māyā* vexes only those who are willing to consider the possibility that there is "something more"[19] behind and beyond nature and history. Radhakrishnan attests that "throughout the history of Indian thought, the ideal of a world behind the ordinary world of human strivings, more real and more intangible....has been haunting the Indian race."[20] Else-

16. IC, 86. Abbreviations used for Radhakrishnan's books and articles are listed alphabetically at the beginning of this book.

17. PU, 18.

18. PRSW, Second Series, p. 134.

19. "Something more" is a phrase used by Theodor Markus Mauch, Professor of Religion, Trinity College, Hartford, Connecticut.

20. IP, II, 766.

where he identifies "the one and only problem, whether there is or is not behind the phenomena of nature and the drama of history an unseen spiritual power."[21] In an address in New Delhi on the occasion of the ninety-second birthday celebration of Swami Vivekananda, 21 February 1954, Radhakrishnan said :

> Is this world which is a perpetual procession of events, self-sustaining, self-maintaining, self-established, or is there a Beyond underlying it, unifying it and inspiring it, standing behind it and yet immanent in it ? Is becoming all or is there being behind it ?[22]

It is argued in the fourth chapter that *māyā*[6] means "one-sided dependence" in Radhakrishnan's thought. He generalizes that *becoming* depends on *being* and that the dependence is one-sided. There can be no question but that Radhakrishnan feels the world depends on a "Beyond" which underlies the world. "Religious consciousness," he confesses, "bears testimony to the reality of something behind the visible, a haunting beyond, which both attracts and disturbs."[23] In his autobiographical essay Radhakrishnan personifies this haunting beyond :

> The major decisions of my life have been taken under a sort of guidance. I think, plan, and prepare, and yet when the choice is made, I have a feeling that an invisible hand has been guiding me for purposes other than my own.[24]

The problem of *māyā* is related to the problem of clarifying what is meant by phrases such as "a world behind the ordinary world," "an unseen spiritual power," "a Beyond," "a haunting beyond," "an invisible hand," and "something more."

Do people in India "negate this world" in order to reach an alleged "other world" ? In 1950, Radhakrishnan looked back over the preceding forty-five years and remarked "from the time I was a student, I have heard criticisms made against Indian religions that they are world-negating and that the attitude of our religious men is one of withdrawal from the world"[25] The

21. CIP, 266.
22. OSW, 1952-1959, 283.
23. ERWT, 85.
24. Ferm, ed., *Religion in Transition*, p. 12.
25. Schilpp, ed., p. 65.

careful student of Radhakrishnan's life and thought will note that in 1950 Radhakrishnan was India's Ambassador to the Soviet Union. It could hardly be said that he had withdrawn from the world. However, arriving at a fair and balanced judgment regarding India's alleged "world-negation" and "other-worldliness" is complicated by the fact that Radhakrishnan himself often laments what he elsewhere denies.

On the one hand, he laments India's alleged other-worldliness. In an early article he complains "the people of India are mostly indifferent to the vital concerns of the world."[26] In 1918 he complained "an exaggerated sense of other-worldliness" is "among the national defects which prevent India from rising to her full height."[27] In a lecture before the Royal Society of Arts in London on 30 April 1937, Radhakrishnan declared in the affirmative that "Hindu religion, like all true religion, is essentially 'otherworldly'."[28] In these instances he fuels the fire of criticism that Indians are world-negating and other-worldly.

On the other hand, Radhakrishnan denies India's other-worldliness. Time and again he argues with great conviction that India's other-worldliness is totally false. In the "Preface" to *Indian Philosophy*, volume one, he exclaims "to the modern mind Indian philosophy means two or three 'silly' notions" which include "*māyā*, or the delusiveness of the world."[29] He denies India's other-worldliness in an important address entitled "The Doctrine of *Māyā* : Some Problems" which he delivered in September 1926 before the International Congress of Philosophy hosted by Harvard. He begins the paper : "It is a common belief in the West that Hindu thought regards the world as an illusion we have to escape from"[30] His purpose in the rest of the paper is to show that "such a view is not fair either to the general tendency of Hindu thought or even to Śaṅkara's metaphysics with which the doctrine of *māyā* is associated."[31] In a

26. "Religion and Life," *International Journal of Ethics* 27 (October 1916) : 103.
27. PRT, 221.
28. ERWT, 75.
29. IP, II, 7.
30. E. S. Brightman, ed., *Proceedings of the Sixth International Congress of Philosophy* (New York: Longmans, Green and Company, 1927), p. 683 (hereafter cited as Brightman, ed., *Proceedings*).
31. Ibid.

speech on 24 April 1954 at the opening of a hospital in Ahmedabad, then Vice-President of The Republic of India Sarvepalli Radhakrishnan proclaimed :

> There is a queer view that the outlook of this nation is other-worldly, not this-worldly, it is world-negating and not world-affirming, that we despise the world as an illusion and concentrate on things above. There cannot be a graver or more erroneous misconception.[32]

World-negation and illusionism are denied again in Radhakrishnan's important "Introduction" to his translation of *The Brahma Sūtra* where he states: "the world is not a deceptive facade of something underlying it."[33] Countering the complaint regarding India's alleged world-negation in a speech delivered in 1966, then President Radhakrishnan pointed out that India has many doctrines other than *advaita vedānta* and that "even *advaita vedānta* does not bring you down to the dismissal of the world as a mere illusion or phantasmagoria."[34] Elsewhere in a discussion of the question "Is the world an illusion' ?" Radhakrishnan presents what he calls "certain considerations which support the phenomenal as against the illusory character of the world."[35] Further evidence could be given to support the conclusion that Radhakrishnan denies India's other-worldliness. Clearly, the problem of *māyā* plagued Radhakrishnan throughout his life.

The question of Hinduism's alleged other-worldliness is related to the question of ethics. If the world is *māyā*, and if *māyā* is interpreted to mean *illusion*, how would ethical seriousness be possible ? If one's interest is directed toward a world other than the world given in the perceptual mode of presentational immediacy, why should one's actions in this world be taken seriously ? In his lecture before the Royal Society of Arts in 1937, Radhakrishnan confronted directly the problem of "Mysticism and Ethics in Hindu Thought." The lecture is a running refutation of Albert Schweitzer's views published in the preceding year in

32. OSW, 1952-1959, 415.
33. BS, 156.
34. PRSW, Second Series, 228. The speech is reprinted as part of "The Legacy of Sanskrit," *Our Heritage* (Delhi: Hind Pocket Books, 1973; an Orient Paperback), pp. 33-38.
35. IP, II, 581.

Indian Thought and Its Development. Radhakrishnan focuses on Schweitzer's book not because he thinks Schweitzer is an authority on Indian thought but because he thinks Schweitzer presents a succinct summary of the charge that Hinduism lacks ethical seriousness. Radhakrishnan says that Schweitzer's argument "is based mainly on the antagonism of the two attitudes which he calls 'world and life affirmation' and 'world and life negation'."[36] Schweitzer identifies the former attitude with Christianity and the latter attitude with Hinduism. Incidentally, Schweitzer's own world-affirming presupposition of the "will to live" comes to mind. Radhakrishnan claims that Heiler "indirectly supports Schweitzer's contention that Indian religion, which is predominantly mystical, is other-worldly and life-denying."[37] In the Upton Lectures at Manchester College, Oxford, delivered in 1926 and published as *The Hindu View of Life*, Radhakrishnan begins an exposition of "Hindu Dharma" with a refutation of the illusionist interpretation of *māyā* :

> Before we turn to the practical side of Hinduism, it is necessary to clear the ground by referring to some of the chief objections urged against the conception of Hindu ethics. The doctrine of *māyā* is supposed to repudiate the reality of the world and thus make all ethical relations meaningless.[38]

The problem is that if the world is illusory, ethical seriousness is laughable. One could assert with justification that the sole purpose for Radhakrishnan's non-illusionist interpretation of *māyā* is to reject other-worldliness in favor of this-worldly action. Radhakrishnan's position is clear: "it is wrong to interpret the meaning of the doctrine of *māyā* in a way that affects the urgency of the ethical demand."[39] In one of his last books he reports : "It is said that against the sole reality of divine being and the paramount need to realize it all the rational and ethical effort involved in the human struggle is ultimately unreal and unsubstantial."[40] However, Radhakrishnan does not share the view

36. ERWT, 65.
37. Ibid., 66.
38. HVL, 45.
39. Ferm, ed., *Religion in Transition*, p. 22.
40. PCF, 21.

that ethical effort and human struggle are unreal. Incidentally, neither does Aurobindo Ghose. But one wonders whether a comparison of Śrī Aurobindo's long years as a recluse in Pondicherry with Radhakrishnan's long years as a public servant in the "world beyond the walls" does not indicate an important difference in the degree to which these two intellectual giants of modern India were committed to ethical action in the secular world.

The ecstasy of divine realization can tempt one to disregard the secular world. Mystical union can lead to an attitude of other-worldliness. Perversion in things religious can begin when religious experience becomes a substitute for moral action. In a discussion of Buddhism and the implications of *karma*, Radhakrishnan refers to the Buddha's warning that the conception of an infinite beyond is a metaphysical fiction: "This warning was needed at a time when people were losing their moral energy in the ecstatic apprehension of the absolute."[41] Elsewhere Radhakrishnan cautions : "the sudden discovery through religious experience of the ultimate reality of spirit inclines us sometimes to look upon the world as an illusion."[42] The same point is made in the first sentence of a section entitled "The Status of the World: *māyā* and *avidyā*" in Radhakrishnan's "Introduction" to his translation of *The Principal Upaniṣads*: "The ecstasy of divine union, the bliss of realisation tempts one to disregard the world with its imperfection and look upon it as a troubled and unhappy dream."[43] Clearly, Radhakrishnan is deeply bothered by Schweitzer's argument that "the empahasis on ecstasy in Hindu thought naturally tends to world and life negation."[44] Radhakrishnan's re-examination of the meanings of *māyā* in his own Hindu tradition is motivated in part by his exposure to arguments like these coming from thinkers in the so-called first world whom he otherwise admires.

Is the doctrine of *māyā* an essential feature or an accidental accretion of *advaita vedānta* and the Hindu tradition ? Among Radhakrishnan's first publications is an article written in 1914

41. IP, I, 458.
42. BG, 38.
43. PU, 78.
44. ERWT, 76.

entitled "The Vedānta Philosophy and the Doctrine of Māyā." It deals at length with the place of *māyā* in Hindu thought, beginning "The doctrine of Maya is considered by many thinkers, both in the East and the West, to be an integral part of the Vedanta philosophy."[45] In 1914 he had published an article on the *vedānta* and ethics, and three years earlier his article on the ethics of the *Bhagavadgītā* and Kant was already published. Radhakrishnan's very first publication was his thesis submitted in 1908 for the M.A. degree from Madras University. The title of his thesis was "The Ethics of the Vedānta and Its Metaphysical Presuppositions." It is reasonable to conclude that in 1914 the twenty-six year old assistant professor of philosophy at Madras Presidency College was genuinely concerned about the doctrine of *māyā*, its place in *vedānta* philosophy, and its implications for ethics.

In the article on *vedānta* philosophy and *māyā* (1914), Radhakrishnan reports :

> Although the doctrine of Maya is viewed at the present day as an essential part of the Vedanta system, Oriental scholars are divided in their opinions concerning the relation of the Maya doctrine to the Vedanta system of philosophy. Mr. Gough, Dr. Deussen of Kiel, and Dr. Prabhu Dutt Shastri have all asserted that the doctrine of Maya is native to the Vedanta philosophy......But, on the other side, Colebrooke and Dr. Thibaut hold that it is a graft of a later growth.[46]

In a word, Radhakrishnan questions whether the concept of *māyā* is a later graft or an essential feature of the cumulative tradition of the Hindus. After examining both positions he tends to support Colebrooke and Thibaut who hold that the doctrine of *māyā* is a later accretion. Prabhu Dutt Shastri and Paul Deussen hold the opposite view. They argue that the illusional interpretation of *māyā* is an essential feature of Hinduism. Referring to the many people in India who are attracted to Śaṁkara's *advaita vedānta*, Prabhu Dutt Shastri declares: "the doctrine of

45. "The Vedānta Philosophy and the Doctrine of Māyā," *International Journal of Ethics* 24 (July 1914): 431. Cited hereafter as "The VP and the DM."

46. "The VP and the DM," 431-432.

Māyā is the foundation-stone on which they rear the whole superstructure of their philosophy of life."[47] The view that *māyā* is central in the day-to-day struggles of the people in India is confirmed by Professor Sinari of the University of Bombay who writes :

> The notion of *māyā* is a point around which the philosophical thought in India has ever revolved. At some stage or other in his life, an Indian makes it a point to brush aside a frustrating experience, a hopelessly incurable situation, even the day-to-day fact of existence, as perishable *māyā*. With the passage of time and with the ever stable impact of the Upaniṣadic *Weltanschauung* on the Indian mind, the word has acquired so popular and persuasive a usage that most often in the Indians' life and literature both poverty and richness, sickness and health, failure and success, danger and safety, death and life, are banished indiscriminately as merely diverse facets of *māyā*.[48]

While Professor Deussen at the University of Kiel was hardly in a geographical position to judge whether the doctrine of *māyā* was central in the lives of Indians, his careful exegesis of the sacred books of the East led him to the conclusion, according to Radhakrishnan, "that the Upaniṣads support the doctrine of *māyā* in the sense of the illusoriness of the world."[49] Radhakrishnan disagrees. The problem is to see how and why.

III. Prabhu Dutt Shastri's Interpretation of Māyā

In *The Doctrine of Māyā*, published in 1911, Prabhu Dutt Shastri gives an interpretation of *māyā* to which Radhakrishnan refers in his article (1914). If the word "orthodox" has any meaning in a Hindu context, Shastri's position regarding *māyā* would be

47. Prabhu Dutt Shastri, *The Doctrin of Māyā in the Philosophy of the Vedānta* (London: Luzac and Company, 1911), p. 109.

48. Ramakant A. Sinari, *The Structure of Indian Thought* (Springfield, Illinois: Charles C. Thomas, 1970), p. 131.

49. IP, I, 188-189.

considered the "orthodox" *advaita vedānta* position. Radhakrishnan's position would be considered "unorthodox." If the words "fundamentalist" and "modernist" could be used non-pejoratively, Shastri could be described as the fundamentalist and Radhakrishnan as the modernist. In order to explicate further the problem under investigation we will consider six of Shastri's main points.

First, Shastri makes the point that the *conception* of *māyā* is much older than the *word māyā*. In his "Preface" to *The Doctrine of Māyā* (p. ix) he announces :

> My conclusions are (1) that the *conception* of *Māyā* is as old as some of the later books of the Ṛgveda... (2) that the *word* '*Māyā*', in the sense of 'illusion' of course, occurs later—for the first time in the Śvetāśvatara Upaniṣad (iv.10).

Throughout the first part of this book Shastri argues in great detail that "the *idea* of *Māyā* is very old—certainly older than the *word māyā*."[50] In short, Shastri's position is that the doctrine of *māyā* precedes the word which expresses it. Radhakrishnan disagrees. Radhakrishnan argues that the early *rishis* were totally free from the encumbrances of tradition and that they said exactly what they meant. His position is that some followers of Śaṅkara read into the Upaniṣads a doctrine of *māyā* which the Upaniṣads do not contain. If the early *rishis* had in mind a concept of *māyā* in the sense of illusion, asks Radhakrishnan, why would they have hesitated to use the word *māyā* to express their alleged view that the world is an illusion ?

Second, Shastri makes a related point about the *Brahma Sūtra*. In a discussion of the *vedānta* system he reports : "The Sūtras, (aphorisms, condensed formulas) which constitute this system are called the *Brahma-Sūtras* or the *Vedānta-Sūtras*, and are 555 in number. The word *māyā*, however, occurs only in one of these (iii.2.3)."[51] Shastri implies, by underlining *word*, that while the *word māyā* occurs just once in 555 *sūtras*, the *conception* of *māyā* occurs much more often. In the concluding paragraph of his chapter on the *Vedānta Sūtra* in *Indian Philosophy*, volume two, Radhakrishnan writes :

> The *Sūtra* of Bādarāyaṇa reflects the indecision and vague-

50. *The Doctrine of Māyā*, p. 35.
51. Ibid., p. 23.

> ness characteristic of the Upaniṣads, whose teachings it attempts to set forth, and harbours within it many seeds of doubt and discussion. ...We shall see in the sequel how identical formulas give rise to various interpretations through the differences of spiritual setting into which they are received.[52]

If Radhakrishnan is correct that the *Brahma Sūtra* is indecisive and vague in general, and if the word *māyā* occurs in just one of its 555 *sūtras*, as Shastri reports, then it is an understatement to say that the *Brahma Sūtra* helps very little in articulating a decisive, clear interpretation of *māyā*.

Third, Shastri makes a point about the meaning of the word *māyā*. He argues that it evolved until the time of Śaṅkara when the meaning *illusion* was established :

> To sum up : we have seen that the word 'māyā' meant in R.V.—
>
> (1) supernatural power, mysterious will-power, wonderful skill, and that the idea of the underlying mystery being more emphasized later on, it came to mean in A.V.
>
> (2) magic, illusion. And, further, we saw that in the Brāhmaṇas and the Upaniṣads also it meant.
>
> (3) illusion, and that this meaning was more and more fixed subsequently, till in the time of Śaṅkara it was established beyond doubt. The sense of 'illusion' may easily be found to exist in form even in the Vedic usage of the term, e.g., where in the R.V. it meant 'power or skill' it always meant 'supernatural' or 'wondrous' power and not the ordinary physical power.[53]

Shastri is thoroughly convinced by his examination of Vedic tradition that *māyā* in the sense of illusion is a matter of record. Before the time of Śaṅkara, says Shastri, the word came to mean illusion. After the time of Śaṅkara, says Shastri, "there has not been any desire to change the meaning of the term by a different usage. Hence it will hardly be of much use to examine the later Sanskrit texts on the Vedānta in order to find out the word

52. IP, II, 444.
53. Shastri, *The Doctrine of Māyā*, p. 31.

'*māyā*'."[54] The clear implication of Shastri's statement is that the entire range of medieval Hinduism is unimportant for interpreting *māyā*. To the contrary, Radhakrishnan thinks that the medieval commentaries deserve careful study. Rather than skipping over the medieval period, Radhakrishnan tries to unite the theism of Rāmānuja with Śaṅkara's non-dualist absolutism. Radhakrishnan disagrees with Shastri's view that *illusion* as the meaning of *māyā* was more and more fixed up to the time of Śaṅkara when it was allegedly established beyond all doubt.

Fourth, Shastri makes a point which Radhakrishnan refutes time and again. He contends that Shastri and others use faulty logic in arguing for an illusional interpretation of *māyā*. Referring to the theory of *māyā*, Shastri contends :

> The theory may be enunciated in two ways : (1) That the world is an illusion or appearance, and (2) That the only reality is the Ātman. These two statements mean the same thing, so that the passages which emphasize the statement that the Ātman is the only reality mean most transparently that all else (i.e., other than the Ātman, viz., the world, etc.) is not real.[55]

Radhakrishnan rejects this contention that the statements "the sole reality is Ātman" and "the world is an illusion" mean the same thing. Radhakrishnan agrees wholeheartedly that the sole reality is Ātman. He agrees wholeheartedly with *advaita vedāntins* that Ātman is Brahman. However, he finds fault with logic which implies that since Brahman (or Ātman) is the sole reality, all else including the world is unreal. Radhakrishnan's reasoning is simple. He suggests that the reality to which the word "Brahman" points is not an exclusive reality. Rather, he claims, it is an inclusive reality; Brahman includes the reality of the world. Therefore, in Radhakrishnan's view, the logic enunciated by Shastri, logic which *advaita vedāntins* have accepted since it was announced by Śaṅkara, is faulty to the core. The details of Radhakrishnan's argument on this matter of faulty logic are important for understanding his interpretation of *māyā*.

54. Ibid., p. 26.
55. Ibid., p. 49.

Fifth, Shastri points to the alleged importance of the Sanskrit particle *iva* which is usually translated "as it were." He says it is so important that it should be supplied in almost all Upaniṣadic passages which refer to that which is other than Brahman, namely, the multiplicity, the diversity, the plurality. For example, *Bṛhad-āraṇyaka Upaniṣad* iv.4.19 describes the destiny of the soul not liberated from *karma-saṃsāra* . "It" in the first two *pādas* refers to Brahman :

> Only by the mind is it to be perceived. In it there is no diversity. He goes from death to death, who sees in it, as it were, diversity.[56]

Discussing this verse, Shastri writes :

> The conception of Māyā exhibits itself in such passages clearly, and yet many do not see it. Here also attention may specially be drawn to the word *iva*—'as it were'—which implies that the multiplicity is only an *appearance*, an 'as it were.' Truly speaking, this 'as it were' should be supplied in almost all passages where the Upaniṣads speak of 'the other.'[57]

Objective analysis of *Bṛhad-āraṇyaka Upaniṣad* iv.4.19 renders it fair to ask why the conception of *māyā* is "clearly" present, as Shastri claims, when the word *māyā* is clearly absent. Furthermore, why should the Upaniṣads be rewritten, as Shastri suggests, by inserting the particle *iva* with its allegedly illusional implication of *māyā* ? What justifies such eisegetical tampering with the text ? Radhakrishnan's interpretation of *māyā* challenges the traditional *advaita vedānta* view of *māyā* by rejecting eisegetical analysis of the Upaniṣads. This study describes and evaluates Radhakrishnan's challenge.

Sixth and finally, Shastri argues that philosophical realism in the Upaniṣads is nothing more than a "concession to the empirical consciousness which refuses to part with the idea of the reality of the world."[58] He claims philosophical realism is a device used by Upaniṣadic sages to satisfy the gross instincts of

56. **Radhakrishnan's translation of B.U. iv.4.19, in P.U. 277.**

57. Shastri, *The Doctrine of Māyā*, p. 56.

58. Ibid., p. 68.

common people. Shastri assumes that idealists belong on high pedestals. He writes :

> In this way for accommodating the real truth of the sole reality of the Ātman (and consequently the falsity of the world) to the empirical consciousness which refuses to part with the grosser conception of the world—an idea with which it has long been familiar—the idealist has to come down from his high pedestal and speak in words intelligible to people in general."[59]

In his article on *māyā* and *vedānta* philosophy (1914), Radhakrishnan quotes some of Shastri's claims regarding alleged "concessions to the empirical consciousness." He disagrees with Shastri :

> If the realistic conception of the universe is merely a concession to the views of the ignorant multitude, it is not easy to see why it is emphasized again and again, in almost every Upanishad. The Upanishad writers, who were wholly untrammelled by authority, cannot be supposed to have laid stress on a strictly untenable position, if it appeared untenable to them.[60]

Radhakrishnan and Shastri are both idealists. The issue is not idealism versus realism. The issue is whether Upaniṣadic *rishis* said what they meant and meant what they said. Should interpreters of the Upaniṣads see what they read and read what they see or should they see what they want to read and read what they want to see? Radhakrishnan asks why the *rishis* would have stressed one thing, in this case a realistic conception of the universe, when they really meant something else. If there is philosophical realism in the Upaniṣads, he contends, it cannot be dismissed as an insignificant concession to empirical consciousness.

59. Ibid., p. 74.
60. "The VP and the DM," 438-439.

IV. Radhakrishnan's Approach to the Problem of Māyā

The general thesis of this study is that as a Hindu modernist, Sarvepalli Radhakrishnan (1) rejects an interpretation of *māyā* which says that the world is an illusion, and (2) accepts an interpretation of *māyā* which says that the term *māyā* has six other meanings. Chapters four and five, respectively, describe and evaluate these six meanings of *māyā* : *māyā*¹ as inexplicable mystery, *māyā*² as power of self-becoming, *māyā*³ as duality of consciousness (*puruṣa*) and matter (*prakṛti*), *māyā*⁴ as primal matter, *māyā*⁵ as concealment, and *māyā*⁶ as one-sided dependence. Chapters two and three, respectively, examine Radhakrishnan's philosophical and religious thought. This final section of chapter one invites the reader to consider Radhakrishnan's general approach to the problem of *māyā*.

One characteristic of Radhakrishnan's approach to the problem of *māyā* is that he dares to differ from tradition. He is not afraid to put forth his own views. In a word, he is a Hindu modernist. After *Indian Philosophy*, volume one, was published in 1923, sympathetic critics sent Radhakrishnan their suggestions. When the second edition of volume one appeared in 1929, Radhakrishnan responded to their criticisms in an appendix entitled "Further Considerations of Some Problems." There he remarks :

> Many of my critics were puzzled by my discussion of the Upaniṣads, since I did not fly a banner and fix a label to my view. My criticism of the theory of 'illusion,' generally associated with Śaṁkara's metaphysics and supported by Deussen, led some of my critics to imagine that I was opposed to Śaṁkara's view. My indifference to personal theism made it equally clear to some others that I was not friendly to Rāmānuja's interpretation. But if one is not a follower of Śaṁkara or of Rāmānuja or any other classical interpreter, it is assumed that one can only be a reveller in strange unphilosophical confusion. I submit that my interpretation of the Upaniṣads is not an unreasonable one, though it may seem to differ from this or that tradition in this or that point.[61]

61. IP, I, 674.

Radhakrishnan insists on the right to differ from tradition. He does not alter his judgments regarding the theory of illusion in order to appease his critics. He does not deny that his views differ from Śaṅkara's and Rāmānuja's. He *does* deny that one who differs from tradition can only be a reveler in strange unphilosophical confusion. In the "Preface" to *Indian Philosophy*, volume one, Radhakrishnan comments on the need to decide among commentators whose interpretations of texts differ :

> One cannot stand silently by without offering some judgment on the conflict of views. Such personal expressions of opinion, however dangerous, can hardly be avoided. Effective exposition means criticism and evaluation.[62]

Conflicts of opinions exist; personal opinions are required. One might ask : "Other than tradition, what criteria does a modernist use to resolve conflicts and shape personal opinions ?" Radhakrishnan deals with this issue in his well-known statement: "while the dominant feature of Eastern thought is its insistence on creative intuition, the Western systems are generally characterised by a greater adherence to critical intelligence."[63] As a builder of bridges between East and West, Radhakrishnan uses *both* creative intuition *and* critical intelligence in daring to differ from tradition.

Radhakrishnan approaches the problem of *māyā* by emphasizing the need for *both* thought *and* action, *both* words *and* deeds. His articles and books contain many variations on this theme. In an article on ethics (1911) in the *Bhagavadgītā* and Kant, Radhakrishnan offers arguments against living in quiet reverie. He contends : "Life is action and action must go on."[64] In an article entitled "Religion and Life," (1916) Radhakrishnan gives the following advice to India which he so dearly loved : "To her we say let your spirituality express itself in the world of facts and action."[65] Elsewhere in the article he recommends : "This organic relationship between the religious spirit and active

62. Ibid., 9.
63. IVL, 129.
64. "The Ethics of the *Bhagavadgītā* and Kant," *International Journal of Ethics* 21 (July 1911): 475.
65. "Religion and Life," *International Journal of Ethics* 27 (October 1916): 106.

life should, in no uncertain voice, be announced to the people of India who are labouring under a false impression."[66] He gives further advice : "Let then the leisureliness and mysticism of the east give place to practical and social idealism."[67] In the Kamala Lectures at the University of Calcutta (1942), Radhakrishnan exclaimed : "Life in the world is not a distraction from, but a means to the attainment of the final end."[68] In his important "Introduction" to his translation of the *Bhagavadgītā*, Radhakrishnan explains and admonishes :

> It is incorrect to assume that Hindu thought strained excessively after the unattainable and was guilty of indifference to the problems of the world. We cannot lose ourselves in inner piety when the poor die at our doors, naked and hungry. The *Gītā* asks us to live in the world and save it.[69]

During May 1944 Radhakrishnan gave lectures in China. In one of these lectures he declared : "Ideas move the world. Thought precedes action."[70] This might be taken to mean that thought is more important than action. However, if thought precedes action, the clear implication is that action must follow thought. This interpretation of Radhakrishnan's position on the relationship between thought and action is confirmed in his Kamala Lectures :

> Thought is the essence of action...all interpretations are intended to change the world. Life is governed by ideals, and philosophies are at the back of all revolutionary movements. What we are is the result of what we think. Philosophers are the creators of the future. The task of philosophy is not merely to interpret life, but to illumine and guide it. Contemplation and life are distincts, not opposites. They can exist together. They imply each other and work together.[71]

The reader will not be surprised to discover that this statement

66. Ibid., p. 102.
67. Ibid., p. 105.
68. RS, 103.
69. BG, 67.
70. IC, 2.
71. RS, 70.

appears in the context of a discussion of Marx. Radhakrishnan contends that thought and action are inseparable, that contemplation and life are not opposed. His view is that they work together. Time and again Radhakrishnan berates what he calls "false asceticism which regards life as a dream and the world as an illusion."[72] In Radhakrishnan's opinion, ascetics make a mistake when they escape into the wilderness to leave behind the worries of the world.[73] In a vivid, well-known image, Radhakrishnan compares ascetics to "cut flowers in metal vases. They are beautiful to contemplate for a while but they soon wither, being without nourishment from the soil."[74] Radhakrishnan's judgment regarding the mendicant ascetics who wander all over the Indian subcontinent is that "these are not the true representatives of the genius of India, who, with a perception of the unity of things (*ekatvam anupaśyati*), move at ease in the world of spirit and the world of sense."[75] Elsewhere, Radhakrishnan describes human perfection as "a sort of marriage between high thought and just action."[76] Again and again this chord is sounded. Thought and action belong together. The world is not an illusion; act in the world ! As Radhakrishnan states quite correctly: "We should develop the spiritual or transcendental attitude which is the very heart of religion, and in that spirit move and live in the world of life and sense."[77] Many more examples from Radhakrishnan's writings could be cited and analyzed. It seems quite clear, however, that Radhakrishnan wants Indians and all others *both* to think *and* to act, *both* to speak *and* to do.

Radhakrishnan approaches the problem of *māyā* by conceiving reality in four poises : (1) *Brahman* (the absolute); (2) *Īśvara* (the personal deity); (3) *Hiraṇyagarbha* (the world-spirit); and (4) *Virāṭ* (the world). His concept of reality in four poises is examined more closely in chapter two, section four. The word "poise" derives from the French *poids* meaning *weight*. Figura-

72. IP, I, 219.
73. HH, 54.
74. EWR, 139.
75. ERWT, 109.
76. BG, 383.
77. RWN, 28.

tively *poise* means "balance, equilibrium, steadiness, stability" or "the condition of being equally balanced between alternatives."[78] Hence, Radhakrishnan gives equal "weight" to each of the four aspects of reality including *Virāṭ*, the world.

The concept of supreme reality in four poises, this study suggests, is the most basic concept in Radhakrishnan's mature hermeneutics. This position is supported by Radhakrishnan's own candid confession :

> As to why the Supreme has this fourfold character, why it is what it is, we can only accept it as the given reality. It is the ultimate irrationality in the sense that no logical derivation of the given is possible. It is apprehended by us in spiritual consciousness, and accounts for the nature of experience in all its aspects. It is the only philosophical explanation that is possible or necessary.[79]

This statement seems to emerge as a *locus classicus* for understanding Radhakrishnan's thought. Nowhere else in all of his writings, this study suggests, does he set forth his basic philosophical and religious assumptions so clearly and distinctly. Some scholars may disagree, arguing that the more traditional, orthodox non-dualism and absolute idealism are Radhakrishnan's foundational ideas. Non-dualism and absolute idealism are certainly central to Radhakrishnan's arguments in two early books—*The Philosophy of Rabindranath Tagore* (1918) and *The Reign of Religion in Contemporary Philosophy* (1920). But as he matures, he loses his unbridled enthusiasm for absolutism and monism. For instance, the word "absolute" is replaced by the word "spirit" as his books unfold during the 1920's and 1930's. The mature Radhakrishnan continues to expound idealism as opposed to realism. However, the mature Radhakrishnan becomes less interested in defending traditional labels like "absolute idealism" and becomes more interested in presenting a positive, systematic theology which reflects fresh insights from his own experience and research.

78. *The Oxford English Dictionary*, 12 vols. (Oxford: Clarendon Press, 1953), s.v. "poise."

79. PU, 90.

How is Radhakrishnan's concept of reality in four poises related to his interpretation of *māyā*? In *The Principal Upaniṣads*, at the end of a long and involved section entitled "The Status of the World: *māyā* and *avidyā*," Radhakrishnan writes : "If we keep in mind the fourfold character of the Supreme, we shall avoid confusion in regard to the status of the world."[80] This confusion *in regard to the status of the world* is the confusion which gives rise to the problem of *māyā*. This confusion can be avoided, Radhakrishnan suggests, by conceiving reality in four poises. Poise one is the *advaita vedānta* absolute (Brahman) and poise four is the world (*Virāṭ*). While the world may not be quite as real as Brahman, argues Radhakrishnan, the world is nevertheless real. The world is not an illusion, he protests, because no poise of supreme reality is an illusion.

Radhakrishnan approaches the problem of *māyā* by rejecting what he contends is faulty logic. He sees no logical necessity in the traditional *advaita vedānta* argument that Brahman is the sole reality and that the world is therefore unreal. He writes : "The first argument used in support of the 'illusion' hypothesis is that the Upaniṣads assert the sole reality of Brahman. It follows that the world is unreal."[81] Does this really follow? Radhakrishnan answers emphatically in the negative. He writes :

> The inference of the unreality of the world from the sole reality of Brahman is legitimate, if the world is viewed as separate from Brahman. But is there any ground for such an assumption? The defenders of the Maya theory assume that the world is something different from Brahman; they combine with this assumption the premise that Brahman alone is real; but we dispute the truth of the other premise that the world is something different from Brahman. The reality of Brahman according to the Vedanta is not exclusive of the reality of the universe... The reality of Brahman everywhere asserted in the Upanishads, instead of implying the unreality of the world, logically involves its reality.[82]

80. Ibid.
81. IP, I, 190.
82. "The VP and the DM," 445.

Radhakrishnan agrees that Brahman is the sole reality. But, he asks, where do the Upaniṣads say that Brahman is *exclusive* of the world ? He portrays Brahman as *inclusive* reality. If Radhakrishnan's Upaniṣadic hermeneutics can be supported, "the unreality of the world" is indeed an illegitimate inference from "the sole reality of Brahman." Radhakrishnan explains : "The Vedanta philosophy does not dispute the reality of the world, but simply declares that the world is not unconditioned."[83] It will be argued in chapter four that Radhakrishnan interprets *māyā*[6] to mean "one-sided dependence." He thinks that Brahman is unconditioned and independent whereas the world is conditioned and dependent. Elsewhere Radhakrishnan complains : "Immediately by a false turn in logic, the spiritual and the ideal is opposed to the human and the natural."[84] Introducing *The Brahma Sūtra*, Radhakrishnan reasons : "The texts that speak of the world as being made up of names and shapes do not lead to the view that *Brahman* alone is real and the world is an appearance."[85] His words "do not lead" suggest that Radhakrishnan has in mind what he considers to be the faulty logic of the illusional interpretation of *māyā*. Elsewhere Radhakrishnan observes: "The hasty logic which declares because the one is real, the many are an illusion, is corrected in the view that the one reveals itself in the many."[86] Incidentally, this statement gives a glimpse of Radhakrishnan's theory of emanation.

Radhakrishnan rejects the illusionist interpretation of *māyā* by a process of elimination. He contends that the word *māyā* has six meanings, none of which is "illusion." By no means does he eliminate the other meanings of *māyā* which, in his view, have accumulated over many centuries of Hindu tradition. However, he does eliminate the meaning "illusion." In his China lectures during 1944, Radhakrishnan recounted a well-known incident in the *Analects* :

> When a disciple asked Confucius what he would consider the first thing to be done, if entrusted with the government of

83. Ibid., 444.
84. "Religion and Life," *International Journal of Ethics* 27 (October 1916): 94.
85. BS, 85.
86. IVL, 110.

> a State, Confucius' reply was : 'the correct definition of names', the fixing of the meanings of words.[87]

Confucius values highly what has come to be called the rectification of names. This study is, in some ways, a rectification of the name *māyā*. Referring to some of the meanings of *māyā* in the *Śvetāśvatara Upaniṣad*, Radhakrishnan writes : "These different significations are not irreconcilable, though confusion will result if we do not carefully distinguish them."[88] The purpose of this book is to eliminate past confusion and to help prevent future confusion by distinguishing carefully among the different significations of the word *māyā*. In the "Preface" to *History of Philosophy, East and West*, volume one, Radhakrishnan refers to the problems of translation :

> Philosophical systems that have arisen in different cultural traditions cannot be compared easily. There are categories in one tradition for which it is difficult to find adequate equivalents in another. The concepts signified by *ātman* and *māyā* are very inadequately rendered by self and illusion or appearance.[89]

Problems of translation in comparative philosophy will not disappear overnight. However, it is hoped that by clarifying Radhakrishnan's rendering of *māyā* this work will contribute something not only to the philosophical dialogue between Hindus and non-Hindus but also to the philosophical dialogue among Hindus who adhere to different *darśanas*.

Radhakrishnan approaches the problem of *māyā* by splitting reality into at least two ontological levels. We have seen that he asks again and again whether there is or is not behind the phenomena of nature and the drama of history an unseen spiritual power. Is there a "Beyond ?" Is there "something more"? Radhakrishnan answers emphatically in the affirmative. He contends that reality is of two kinds: absolute reality and reality which is not absolute. Radhakrishnan uses at least nine adjectives to describe reality which is not absolute : conditioned,

87. IC, 64.
88. IP, I, 513.
89. HPEW, I, 6.

contingent, created, dependent, empirical, finite, manifested, phenomenal, and relative. In various contexts, Radhakrishnan's bifurcation of reality is indicated by one or more of these adjectives. Incidentally, the early Radhakrishnan often refers to the whole and its parts. Here, too, reality is being split. There can be no doubt that Radhakrishnan's splitting of reality into two levels is related to his interpretation of *māyā*. He writes: "The Upaniṣads support the doctrine of māyā only in the sense that there is an underlying reality containing all elements from the personal God to the telegraph post."[90] This *underlying reality* is what he refers to elsewhere with the phrases *unseen spiritual power* and *a beyond*. The following affirmation by Radhakrishnan raises a related issue : "it is an accepted canon of metaphysical criticism that what is not at the beginning or end cannot be said to be really in its present process. Plurality may be actual or existent, but it is not real."[91] Radhakrishnan presupposes the one before and after the plural. But of particular interest is Radhakrishnan's bifurcation of that which is the case into "actuality" and "reality." He contends that the actual and the real are on different ontological levels. It is Radhakrishnan's position that the "actual" is conditioned, contingent, created, dependent, empirical, finite, manifested, phenomenal, and relative whereas the "real" is none of these.

Radhakrishnan approaches the problem of *māyā* by distinguishing between phenomenality and unreality. He contends that the phenomenal is neither the real nor the unreal. In *Indian Philosophy*, volume two, he raises the specific question : "Is the world an illusion ?" In his nine page answer Radhakrishnan writes :

> As this view, which makes a tragic joke of life, renders meaningless many statements of Śaṁkara on the world of experience, and does violence to every canon of sound interpretation, we may here bring together certain considerations which support the phenomenal as against the illusory character of the world.[92]

90. IP, I, 197.
91. IP, I, 338.
92. IP, II, 581.

Radhakrishnan correctly contends that the world is phenomenal but not unreal. However, he also contends that the world is phenomenal but not real. This study rejects his argument on this point. Splitting reality into two or more levels is forensically convenient but philosophically unsatisfying. Śaṅkara distinguishes between *vyāvahārika sattā* and *prātibhāsika sattā*. Radhakrishnan accepts Śaṅkara's distinction :

> Of course Śaṁkara affirms that the world is not Brahman. As the manifestation of Brahman it is real only in a secondary sense; it has what is called *vyāvahārika sattā*. By no means is it to be dismissed as utterly unreal. It is different from *prātibhāsika sattā* or illusory existence.[93]

Chapter two of this study examines more carefully this distinction between illusory existence and an alleged level of phenomenal existence between the unreal and the real. The point here is that Radhakrishnan argues against the illusory character of the world by distinguishing between phenomenality and unreality.

Radhakrishnan argues that the reality of the world and the reality of the Absolute-God are radically different. The reality of the world is not absolute, according to Radhakrishnan. He modifies the word *world* with each of the nine adjectives listed above. The reality of Absolute-God *is* absolute, according to Radhakrishnan. He modifies the word *Absolute* with the negative forms of the nine adjectives above. Radhakrishnan explains :

> This world is not an illusion; it is not nothingness, for it is willed by God and therefore real. Its reality is radically different from the being of Absolute-God. The Absolute alone has non-created divine reality; all else is dependent, created reality. This is the significance of the doctrine of *māyā*.[94]

The reality of the world is at a level somewhere between reality which is Absolute-God and unreality. This approach to an understanding of the scheme of things entire might be judged negatively by others. However, Radhakrishnan assesses posi-

93. OSW, 1952-1959, 322.
94. Schilpp, ed., 41.

tively Śaṅkara's position that the world is radically different from Absolute-God.

Radhakrishnan approaches the problem of *māyā* axiologically. He suggests :

> When the Hindu thinkers ask us to free ourselves from *māyā*, they are asking us to shake off our bondage to the unreal values which are dominating us. They do not ask us to treat life as an illusion or be indifferent to the world's welfare.[95]

Unfortunately, the phrase "unreal values" combines axiological and ontological issues. It makes one wonder : "How can a value be unreal?" Nevertheless, this statement about shaking off the bondage to misplaced values expresses Radhakrishnan's conviction that the problem of *māyā* is primarily a problem of values. A reorientation of values is required for soteriological results. This does not imply that the world has no value. Radhakrishnan writes: "earthly life is not to be regarded as illusory or indifferent; it has a positive value for the evolution of the soul."[96] Yet the positive value of earthly life is not ultimate, argues Radhakrishnan. He remarks :

> When we are asked to overcome *māyā*, it is an injunction to avoid worldliness. Let us not put our trust in the things of this world. *Māyā* is concerned not with the existence of the world but with its meaning, not with the factuality of the world but with the way in which we look upon it.[97]

Radhakrishnan is arguing here that the meaning or value of the world, not its existence, is the real problem of *māyā*. Were Radhakrishnan's ontological disclaimer affidavit correct, though, one would have to ask : "Why in Radhakrishnan's writings do discussions of *māyā* contain statements regarding what the world *is* and what the world *is not*?"

Radhakrishnan counters the charge that Indians are otherworldly by reiterating the *Yoga Sūtra's* prescription for developing one's physical condition. Bodily well-being is linked to spiri-

95. ERWT, 47.
96. "Hinduism and the West," in *Modern India and the West*, ed. L. S. S. O'Malley (Oxford: The University Press, 1941), p. 352.
97. PU, 89.

tual success. As Radhakrishnan correctly points out :

> Physical well-being, positive health is an essential prerequisite of any other kind of development, either of spiritual qualities or intellectual powers. The *Yoga-Sūtra* is said to be a science of the development of spiritual powers. But it insists that physical prowess is essential.[98]

Elsewhere[99] Radhakrishnan states that "health or *ārogya* is the basis for all other developments, ethical and economic, artistic and spiritual." Radhakrishnan argues that each of these ethical, economic, artistic and spiritual goals is important in the Hindu worldview. In the "Introduction" to an edition of Kālidāsa's works sponsored by the Sāhitya Akademi, Radhakrishnan states :

> Kālidāsa's writings dispose of the misconception that the Hindu mind was attentive to transcendental matters, and neglectful of mundane affairs. ...He points to a harmony of four main interests of human life, *dharma*, *artha*, *kāma*, and *mokṣa*.[100]

Good health, physical prowess, and beauty of the body are lavishly portrayed in sumptuous sculpture at Khajurāho and Konārak. "Whatever may be the Hindu practice," writes Radhakrishnan, "Hindu religion cannot be regarded as unworldly or otherworldly."[101] An argument for Hindu this-worldliness, illustrated by *Yoga Sūtra* prescriptions for physical conditioning and artistic portrayals of physical pleasure, adds another weapon to Radhakrishnan's arsenal of arguments against the illusional interpretation of *māyā*.

In the long view, Radhakrishnan's most important argument against an illusional interpretation of *māyā* is his argument that the doctrine of *māyā*, in the sense of illusion, is not a tenet of the original *vedānta*. We have already mentioned the importance of Radhakrishnan's article (1914) entitled "The Vedānta Philosophy and The Doctrine of Māyā." Incidentally, this article prompted the research being reported. The article's specific purpose is to show that the doctrine of *māyā* interpreted as illu-

98. PCF, 185.
99. OSW, 1952-1959, 442.
100. Ibid., 563.
101. Ferm, ed., *Religion in Transition*, p. 21.

sion is not a tenet of the original *vedānta.* In the article, Radhakrishnan refers to a paper on *vedānta* read in 1827 by Colebrooke before the Royal Asiatic Society. As we have seen, Colebrooke and Shastri disagree regarding the authenticity of *māyā* in early *vedānta.* Radhakrishnan writes of Colebrooke :

> He is right, according to the present writer [Radhakrishnan], in thinking that the text of the Vedanta, viz., the Vedas, the earlier Upanishads, and Vedanta Sutras does not suggest, even remotely, the theory of Maya. On the other hand, it will be possible for us to establish that these texts point to a realistic conception of the universe. It was Sankara, under the influence of the Buddhistic teaching, following the traditions of Gaudapada, who imported the conception of Maya into the Vedanta system. Maya is a pivotal principle of the later Sankara Vedanta, but it is not a part of the primitive cosmological conception of the Vedas and the earlier Upanishads.[102]

In this statement, Radhakrishnan makes his position perfectly clear. "Maya" in this statement means *māyā* interpreted as "illusion"; it does *not* mean *māyā*[1], *māyā*[2], *māyā*[3], *māyā*[4], *māyā*[5], or *māyā*[6], as explained in chapter four below. Radhakrishnan does not reject these six meanings of *māyā.* The 1914 article contains one of Radhakrishnan's strongest arguments against illusionism as a tenet of original *vedānta.* He reasons : "If the Maya doctrine had really been held by the earlier Vedantins, they would have said something about Maya when the theories of creation were described."[103] It is the case that the Upaniṣads contain several different creation stories. It is also the case that these stories do not contain the word *māyā.* Only by using an argument like Shastri's can one seriously maintain that *māyā* is a significant Upaniṣadic concept. As we have seen, Shastri argues that even though the *word māyā* does not appear in early *vedānta* texts, the *conception* of *māyā* is nevertheless there. It is the purpose of this study to show how and why Radhakrishnan disagrees with Shastri. Shastri never would have agreed with the following statement by Radhakrishnan : "The conclusion

102. "The VP and the DM," 432.
103. Ibid., 447.

at which we arrive is that the doctrine of Maya is not an integral part of the Vedanta system of philosophy."[104]

Radhakrishnan approaches the problem of *māyā* by criticizing Śaṅkara. Referring to the idea of *māyā* in Śaṅkara, Radhakrishnan writes : "I may perhaps develop Śaṁkara's suggestive idea in my own way."[105] Radhakrishnan dares to differ with tradition even when the tradition begins with Śaṅkara. Radhakrishnan provides charitably an explanation for Śaṅkara's mistake : "The anxiety to be loyal as far as possible to both Buddhism and Vedantism appears to be the explanation of much of the inconsistency of Śaṁkara's philosophy."[106] Radhakrishnan then goes on to imply that Śaṅkara's writings are full of passages which contain an incorrect view of the relation between world and Absolute. Radhakrishnan judges :

> Here and there we come across passages where Sankara holds to the right view of the relation between the world and the Absolute. But these have lost their force, as passages pointing to an opposite view are to be met with in almost every page of Śaṁkara's writings, and as the interpreters of Śaṁkara's system have practically ignored it.[107]

Radhakrishnan is saying, in effect, that once in a while Śaṅkara was correct on this issue. Radhakrishnan is also saying that most of the time the interpreters of Śaṅkara's system have overlooked the few places where Śaṅkara holds the correct view of the world's relation to the Absolute. Elsewhere Radhakrishnan criticizes : "It is Śaṁkara's excessive attachment to logical precision that leads him into somewhat misleading statements, to the effect that the world is nought."[108] These misleading statements are denounced by Radhakrishnan even more strongly elsewhere. He would prefer to shift responsibility for illusionism to the Buddhists, but his scholarly objectivity does not allow him to vindicate Śaṅkara completely. After a discussion of views presented by opponents of Śaṅkara who judge that Śaṅkara's *māyāvāda* is Buddhism in disguise, Radhakrishnan writes :

104. Ibid., 451.
105. Brightman, ed., *Proceedings*, p. 685.
106. PRT, 116.
107. Ibid., 117.
108. IP, I, 638.

> All these estimates imply that Śaṁkara incorporated certain Buddhistic elements such as the doctrine of *māyā* and monasticism into the Vedānta philosophy. It is held that, in an endeavour to preserve the continuity of thought, he attempted to combine logically incompatible ideas. However creditable this may be to the elasticity of Śaṁkara's mind or his spirit of genuine toleration, it cannot but affect the logical rigour of his thought; and the theory of *māyā* serves as a cloak to cover the inner rifts of his system.[109]

This statement, if correct, is damaging to Śaṅkara's reputation. However, it damages Śaṅkara's reputation by pointing to just one issue about which Radhakrishnan has complaints. Radhakrishnan agrees with Śaṅkara on so many other issues that this one disagreement regarding the theory of *māyā* cannot hurt Śaṅkara much. It hurts Śaṅkara's reputation only in the eyes of those like Shastri who assert that the theory of *māyā* is the pivotal feature of *vedānta* philosophy. Incidentally, it can be argued persuasively that Radhakrishnan's own systematic theology contains rifts which are caused by the elasticity of *his* own mind and by *his* own zealous espousal of complete toleration.

Radhakrishnan's approach to the problem of *māyā* includes an attempt to unite the views of Śaṅkara and Rāmānuja. In his famous discussion of the philosophy of the Upaniṣads, Radhakrishnan concludes: "It is difficult to decide whether it is the Advaita (or non-dualism) of Śaṁkara, or the modified position of Rāmānuja that is the final teaching of the parent gospel."[110] Radhakrishnan's tendency to rely on Jaina logic inclines him, therefore, to accept interpretations from *both* Śaṅkara *and* Rāmānuja. Reflecting on his own discussion of Upaniṣadic philosophy in *Indian Philosophy*, volume one, Radhakrishnan indicated :

> My endeavor was to show how the Upaniṣads lent themselves to divergent developments and whether it was not possible to give a coherent account of their teaching which would do

109. IP, II, 471-472.

110. IP, I, 258.259.

> justice to the main principles of the two chief interpreters, Śaṁkara and Rāmānuja.[111]

Radhakrishnan intentionally combines their world-views. According to Radhakrishnan, Śaṅkara "regards the absolute as pure being and makes the world an accidental appearance (vivarta) of it" while Rāmānuja "looks upon the absolute as a concrete person of whom the world is the necessary expression."[112] Much later in his career, Radhakrishnan makes another unequivocal statement which indicates that his purpose is to unite the views of Rāmānuja and Śaṅkara :

> R. takes into account Ś.'s views and develops a theistic interpretation with great feeling, vast learning and brilliant logic. Ś. and R. represent two uninterrupted traditions of Indian thought. To my mind these traditions are not exclusive of each other but complementary.[113]

While uniting the views of Śaṅkara and Rāmānuja is not motivated solely by the desire to solve the problem of *māyā*, Radhakrishnan's desire to interpret *māyā* in an acceptable fashion is no doubt a partial reason for the merger.

Radhakrishnan approaches the problem of *māyā* by arguing that most *vedāntins* after Śaṅkara reject the illusional interpretation of *māyā*. The limited scope of this study precludes an examination of the general history of *māyā* interpretations. An unlimited study of *māyā* hermeneutics from the beginning of Hinduism would require a great deal more research than is reported here.[114] For instance, it would have to include a careful examination of Surendranath Dasgupta. But there can be no

111. Ibid., 674.
112. Ibid., 675.
113. BS, 51.
114. Ruth Reyna, *The Concept of Māyā—From the Vedas to the 20th Century* (Bombay and New York: Asia Publishing House, 1962); Anil Kumar Ray Chaudhuri, *The Doctrine of Māyā* (Calcutta: Dasgupta and Company, 1950); P. D. Devanandan, *The Concept of Māyā* (London: Lutterworth Press, 1950); Donald Richard Tuck, "*Māyā*: Interpretative Principle for an Understanding of the Religious Thought of Śaṁkara and Radhakrishnan" (Ph.D. dissertation, The University of Iowa, 1970). L. Thomas O'Neil *Māyā in Śaṅkara : Measuring the Immeasurable* (Columbia, Missouri: South Asia Books; Delhi: Motilal Banarsidass, 1980).

question about Radhakrishnan's position regarding the question "Is the world an illusion?" He concludes a six-page discussion of the doctrine of *māyā* :

> No theory has ever asserted that life is a dream and all experienced events are illusions. One or two later followers of Śaṁkara lend countenance to this hypothesis, but it cannot be regarded as representing the main tendency of Hindu thought.[115]

Radhakrishnan may be overstating his case just a bit because it is generally agreed that Gauḍapāda's dream analysis contains illusionism. But Radhakrishnan's general position is to call for a shift in Hindu paradigms away from "illusion" hermeneutics. The main tendency of Hindu thought seems to be non-illusional. However, the virtually infinite complexity of Hindu thought should scare any student from ever making any statement about "the main tendency" of Hinduism. It is more accurate to say that Hinduism has "main tendencies."

Radhakrishnan was greatly influenced by Rabindranath Tagore's vision of *māyā* and ethics. Radhakrishnan writes autobiographically : "In regard to my views on Hindu ethics and the doctrine of *māyā*, I found great support in the writings or Rabindranath Tagore."[116] Unfortunately, Radhakrishnan's early book *The Philosophy of Rabindranath Tagore* (1918) borders on the panegyric. In it Radhakrishnan defends Tagore from those Hindus who said Tagore had gone Christian. Radhakrishnan writes of Tagore : "He gives us a 'human' God, dismisses with contempt the concept of the world-illusion, praises action overmuch and promises fulness of life to the religious soul."[117] Tagore's romantic relationship with nature prevented him from dismissing the world as an illusion. Referring to medieval India when religion allegedly tended to inspire men and women only to become resigned to their sufferings, Radhakrishnan states: "Rabindranath protests against this world-negating attitude."[118] In a discussion of the dangers of both Western materialism and

115. HVL, 50.
116. Ferm, ed., *Religion in Transition*, p. 23.
117. PRT, 4.
118. Ibid., 222.

Eastern spirituality, Radhakrishnan restates Tagore's judgment :

> The pervading concern for the things of the spirit has led to an unconcern for the things of the world, and we are today reaping the fruits of age-long unconcern and other-worldliness. We have never cared to provide for the great masses of our population the necessary conditions of material existence, indispensable to civilised life.[119]

This study has already pointed out how Radhakrishnan's interpretation of *māyā* is motivated by his desire to inspire positive ethical action in the world.

Finally, Radhakrishnan's approach to the problem of *māyā* is to ignore *māyā* so that interest in it will eventually disappear. Since *māyā* hermeneutics is the focal point of this investigation, the reader may get the impression that *māyā* is also the focal point of Radhakrishnan's thought. This is not the case. Radhakrishnan's articles, books, speeches, and other writings tend to ignore *māyā*. For instance, the first chapter of *The Heart of Hindusthan* (1936) is an article reprinted from *The Hibbert Journal* entitled "The Heart of Hinduism." Radhakrishnan's stated purpose is "to describe, not defend, the central features of the faith of the Hindus."[120] Even though the first section of the chapter contains a description of Hinduism's "Philosophical Basis," it does not mention the doctrine of *māyā*. Below in chapter three we shall investigate the content of Radhakrishnan's faith by examining many passages in which he lists Hinduism's central features. *Māyā* is conspicuous by its absence from these lists. If the result of this exposition of *māyā* in Radhakrishnan's thought is to perpetuate interest in illusional hermeneutics as a central feature of Hinduism, it will have failed utterly.

119. Ibid., 104.
120. HH, 1.

2

Background Concepts in Radhakrishnan's Philosophy

I. Introduction

This chapter presents some background concepts in the philosophy of Sarvepalli Radhakrishnan. Background concepts[1] are the presuppositions, propositions, and root principles which give shape to a particular intellectual architectonic. On 17 November 1958 at the University of Bonn, West Germany, Radhakrishnan delivered an address entitled "The Metaphysical Quest." He concluded : "We need constructive philosophy, an articulation of ultimate pre-suppositions about the world we live in."[2] In Radhakrishnan's system, *māyā* is one such ultimate presupposition about the phenomena of nature and the drama of history. Elsewhere Radhakrishnan proclaims : "It is fairly obvious that the great philosophers admit that the root principles are articles of faith, and not attained by argument."[3] Identifying such root principles in Radhakrishnan's philosophy will facilitate the understanding of his *māyā* hermeneutics. Elsewhere he cautions wisely : "There are certain propositions which are presupposed in experience [and] which can neither be proved nor disproved."[4] Whether they are called ultimate presuppositions, root principles, or propositions, it cannot be denied that

1. cf. Paul Edwards, ed. in chief, *The Encyclopedia of Philosophy* (New York: The Macmillan Company, 1969), vol. 6, s.v. "presupposing."
2. OSW, 1952-1959, 399.
3. IVL, 174.
4. S. Radhakrishnan and J. H. Muirhead, eds., CIP, 268.

philosophical systems display background concepts which can neither be verified nor falsified. Radhakrishnan is not to be criticized for the fact *that* his intellectual architectonic includes unverifiable concepts. He may be criticized only for *what* he asserts without argument.

The next chapter identifies recurring themes in Radhakrishnan's religious faith. Considering the topics of these two chapters, an obvious question arises : "How does the content of his philosophy differ from the content of his religious faith ?" The answer would be easy if we could only identify how Radhakrishnan defines either philosophy or religion.[5] Since the primary purpose of this study is to investigate the place of *māyā* in Radhakrishnan's philosophical and religious thought, we cannot explore the issues raised by his protean approach to definitions.

However, a composite sketch of Radhakrishnan's many-sided definition of philosophy is instructive. Numerous statements throughout his writings begin "Philosophy is..." For instance, Radhakrishnan proclaims that "Philosophy is obviously an *intellectual* attempt to deal with the nature of reality."[6] He underlines "intellectual" in order to emphasize what he calls "method." Stating quite correctly that there is no generally accepted definition of philosophy, Radhakrishnan goes on to suggest that philosophy is "*a logical inquiry into the nature of reality*."[7] Elsewhere he describes philosophy as "the attempt to think out the presuppositions of experience, to grasp. by means of reason, life or reality as a whole."[8] As a recurring theme, the concept of "a whole" is found especially in his early books. For example, he portrays philosophy as "an attempt to conceive the world as a whole by means of thought."[9] Still elesewhere he explains :

Philosophy according to the idealist position is a construc-

5. Referring to D. M. Datta, S. J. Samartha writes: "Datta, discussing primarily Radhakrishnan's interpretation of Indian philosophy, draws attention gently but firmly to 'the intolerable ambiguity' in certain areas of Radhakrishnan's work because of a lack of precision in the use of certain words and an absence of definition of certain key terms," in *Introduction to Radhakrishnan : The Man and His Thought* (New York: Association Press, 1964), p. 106.

6. RRCP, 1.

7. Schilpp, ed., 816.

8. RRCP, 412.

9. PRT, 163.

> tion of experience. The immediate facts of the world, which constitute the starting-point of the philosophic inquiry, are taken up into a synthesis where their immediacy and externality are broken down.[10]

Radhakrishnan will never be mistaken for a philosophical realist as long as he posits the dissolution of the externality of facts. Elsewhere Radhakrishnan defines philosophy as :

> ...a progressive discovery of reality or defining of reality in terms of fundamental conceptions or categories, or a gradual passage from lower, more abstract and indefinite conceptions, to higher, more concrete and definite ones.[11]

According to this definition, the process of discovering "background concepts" would qualify as philosophy. A variation on the recurring theme of "the unseen as a living reality" is contained in Radhakrishnan's reference to philosophy as "a quest of truth which underlies existence."[12] Radhakrishnan's suggestion that "philosophy is not a deductive development of conclusions from set dogmas, but the explication of the presuppositions of experience"[13] contains the rationale for this chapter's explication of background concepts. Finally, Radhakrishnan describes philosophy as "a criticism of categories."[14] This entire project might be viewed as a criticism of one category—*māyā*. Now it is time to ask whether philosophy can be all of these things Radhakrishnan says it is. One could probably construct a complex architectonic showing that elements in each of his definitions of philosophy display Wittgensteinian family resemblances. However, a simpler approach is to accept the fact that Radhakrishnan views philosophy as many-sided. Incidentally, for the purposes of this project philosophy is defined as ongoing, critical reflection on the process of events entire—reflection which begins with wonder, maintains coherence, and results in action.[15]

10. PRT, 134.
11. RRCP, 413.
12. Schilpp, ed., 38.
13. RRCP, 402.
14. PRSW, Second Series, 174. This definition appears elsewhere, RRCP, 413. Other "philosophy is...." statements are scattered throughout Radhakrishnan's writings. See RRCP, 16.
15. The phrase "process of events entire" is intended by the author to

Sir Sarvepalli Radhakrishnan views philosophy as spiritual. He declares : "It is the function of philosophy to provide us with a spiritual rallying centre."[16] In his address to the sixth International Congress of Philosophy at Harvard in 1926, Radhakrishnan described the disappearance of old ideals and continued : "The new ideals have not come into being. Here is the chance for philosophy. Are we to drift, waiting for something to turn up ? Or shall we undertake the spiritual direction of the community ?"[17] That philosophers nurture the spirit-life of humanity is not a generally accepted view in modern Western thought. But Radhakrishnan feels deeply that philosophers should be active advocates of specific ideals. He challenges philosophers to change the world as well as interpret it. His retirement speech illustrates this point. Members of Parliament in New Delhi praised Radhakrishnan lavishly when he retired from the presidency of India in May 1967. In his reply to their farewell address, Radhakrishnan reflected upon the many occasions when people introducing his speeches had referred to Plato's figure of the philosopher-king. Plato's dictum that philosophers should rule the state, argues Radhakrishnan, is common to all great cultures : "All students of philosophy are called upon not merely to interpret but to change the world, not only to exert their vision but also to exert honest service, honest dedication."[18] Radhakrishnan's assumption that philosophical vision and honest service are inextricably intertwined underlay his move into India's presidential residence, Rashtrapati Bhavan. He hoped that honest service and dedication in the public sector would flow from a vision of philosophy as spiritual.

Radhakrishnan's philosophy is Indian idealism. Like all his other definitions, his definition of idealism cannot be stated in one sentence. In his view this is not problematical : "An idealist view of life is not expressed in any one pattern. It is

parallel the more common phrase "scheme of things entire." The new phrase moves philosophy away from the indadequacy of substantialism and towards the process perspective of Whitehead, Hartshorne, D. D. Williams, Cobb, and others.

16. IVL, 83. Cf. "Philosophy in India is essentially spiritual." (IP, I, 24)

17. Brightman, ed., *Proceedings*, 546.

18. PRSW, Second Series, 93.

many-coloured and its forms are varied."[19] The first section of *An Idealist View of Life* is entitled "What is Idealism?" It is the best primary source for Radhakrishnan's particular brand of idealism. He begins by rejecting two views of "idea." An "idea," he says, is not a particular mental image. Neither is it a universal notion. He goes on :

> There is a third sense in which the term 'idea' is used. When we ask with reference to any thing or action, 'what is the idea?' we mean, what is the principle involved in it, what is the meaning or the purpose of its being, what is the aim or value of the action? What is it driving at? This idea or value is the operative creative force. An idealist view finds that the universe has meaning, has value. Ideal values are the dynamic forces, the driving power of the universe. The world is intelligible only as a system of ends.[20]

For Radhakrishnan, ideas or values are operative creative forces, the driving power of the universe. He theorizes that an idea, ideal, or value has teleological efficacy. Incidentally, "idea" and "ideal" are virtually synonymous in Radhakrishnan's usage. His idealism fits the definition given by one of his students :

> We may now define idealism as the theory which asserts the reality of the ideal, and explains the world in order to maintain this conception of reality. This conception may be maintained by explaining the world in terms of the ideal reality, or by saying that the imperfect vanishes or is transformed at the level of the perfect.[21]

The reader's attention is invited to several more illustrations which help clarify the nature of Radhakrishnan's idealism. He declares that "Enlightened ideas have a transforming power."[22] Elsewhere he remarks : "There is, all through, the pressure of an absolute ideal, the control exercised by the nature of reality."[23]

19. IVL, 16.
20. IVL, 14-15.
21. P. T. Raju, *Idealist Thought of India* (London: George Allen and Unwin, 1953), p. 69, cited in Robert A. McDermott, "Radhakrishnan's Comparative Philosophy" (Ph.D. dissertation, Boston University, 1969), p. 7.
22. BS, 136.
23. Brightman, ed., *Proceedings*, 543.

Radhakrishnan's motivation for defending absolute idealism is to preserve the alleged reality of the ideals.[24] His Indian idealism is intended to generate trust in the universe because he is convinced that "There is an ultimate decency in things."[25]

In short, Radhakrishnan sees the need for constructive philosophy, an articulation of ultimate presuppositions about the process of events entire. "Background concepts" are what Radhakrishnan calls presuppositions, root principles, and propositions. To illustrate Radhakrishnan's many-sided definition of philosophy, attention has been invited to statements throughout his writings which begin "Philosophy is..." He identifies philosophy as spiritual and exhorts philosophers to change the world as well as interpret it. Finally, he posits the teleological efficacy of ideals and values which he describes as the operative creative forces of the universe.

II. Epistemological Concepts

Chapter three of *Religion in a Changing World* opens with a discussion of metaphysics in which Radhakrishnan delineates two main fields : ontology and epistemology. The rest of the chapter focuses on ontology and avoids epistemology, indicating the relative importance Radhakrishnan gives to each field. His precise wording of three supposedly epistemological questions is revealing : "What can the human mind know with certainty ? How does opinion differ from knowledge ? What can be known ?"[26] The first and last questions focus on the *content* of knowledge. Radhakrishnan tends to avoid the methodological question "How do we know ?" Elsewhere he states as a central assumption of philosophy that things are not always what they seem.[27] If this is true, we need a method to determine what things are. Radhakrishnan addresses this issue : "Empirical objects may be known by outer observation and inner introspection."[28] But this statement is highly controversial. Generally,

24. RRCP, 432.
25. IVL, 155.
26. RCW, 57.
27. RRCP, 351.
28. PU, 97.

inner introspection is not accepted in modern Western philosophical circles as a means of knowing.

Although a complete study[29] could be devoted to intuition and intellect in Radhakrishnan's thought, this section will consider four background concepts in his epistemology : (1) reality which cannot be grasped by the discursive intellect; (2) intuitive knowledge which operates in a mode of presentational immediacy; (3) the many-sidedness of truth; and (4) some criteria for truth.

First of all, Radhakrishnan contends that reality in its wholeness cannot be grasped by the discursive intellect. He theorizes that the Absolute cannot be known in its entirety,[30] often using theological language to make his point :

> Brahman is unknowable in its entirety, while knowable in part. Reality is neither completely unknown nor completely known. Reality in its wholeness cannot be grasped by the discursive understanding, which distinguishes, separates, and relates. The final unity at which thought aims is beyond all concepts.[31]

Knowledge of the parts is possible; knowledge of the whole is said to be impossible. Particularly noteworthy is the literary and consequently philosophical parallelism of *Brahman*, *reality*, and the *final unity*. Generally speaking, *unity* can be substituted for *Brahman*, *the Absolute*, or *ultimate reality* without changing Radhakrishnan's meaning. Whichever parallel expression he uses, Radhakrishnan definitely thinks "it is impossible, so long as one occupies the logical standpoint, to grasp reality in itself."[32]

29. The best available discussions on Radhakrishnan's epistemology are: (1) J. G. Arapura, *Radhakrishnan and Integral Experience* (Bombay and New York: Asia Publishing House, 1966), esp. his chapter entitled "The Method of Knowledge" in which he discusses "Rational Intuition," "Intuition of Feeling," and "Mystical Intuition"; and (2) R.A. McDermott, "Radhakrishnan's Comparative Philosophy" (Ph.D. dissertation, Boston University, 1969).

30. "The VP and the DM," 442. Cf. "The Absolute unity is opposed to the intellectual duality, and the intellectual account of the Absolute remains a negative one." (PRT, 50).

31. Ibid. Cf. Radhakrishnan's reference to the unknowability of Brahman, IP, I, 234.

32. IP, II, 141.

Incidentally, Śaṅkara's theory of superimposition (*adhyāsa*) is a variation on this general *advaita vedānta* theme that reality in its entirety cannot be grasped. Also, we shall see in chapter four that *māyā*[1]—meaning inexplicable mystery—is not unrelated to this epistemological background concept.

Radhakrishnan takes the position that knowledge of the real is intuitive. He equates intuitive knowledge and integral insight (*anubhava*, from $\sqrt{}$*bhū*+*anu* meaning "that which is come up with, attained"). Radhakrishnan remarks in his autobiography :

> Spiritual certainty is conveyed by spiritual knowledge, which is not merely perceptual or conceptual. This knowledge is not a-logical but super-logical. It is called integral insight or intuitive knowledge.[33]

He uses *spiritual knowledge*, *integral insight*, and *intuitive knowledge* appositionally. That Radhakrishnan equates knowledge and insight is not surprising in that he thinks philosophy is vision (*darśana*, from $\sqrt{}$*dṛś*, "to see," meaning "that which is seen"). Upaniṣadic sages are called *rishis*, those who see. Even though Radhakrishnan thinks reality in its wholeness cannot be grasped by the discursive intellect, intuitive insight into reality is possible. He writes: "The fact of this integral or intuitive knowledge tells us that we are not helplessly shut out from an insight into reality by the constitution of our minds."[34] Clearly, the nature of knowledge is a central issue for East-West philosophical dialogue. Radhakrishnan attests that "non-sensuous, immediate knowledge"[35] is possible. He charges that Kant "misconceived the nature of knowledge by confining it to the physico-mathematical type."[36] Whether Kant's concept of knowledge is more or less confining than Radhakrishnan's is a fascinating issue, but it requires a complete study in itself.

In the second place, Radhakrishnan thinks knowledge is gained by intuition which operates in a mode of presentational immediacy. Discussing Tagore and the relation between

33. Ferm, ed., 36. *Anubhava* is discussed in IP, II, 534; IP, II, 639; PU, 103; IVL, 128; and BS, 108.

34. Ibid., 37. On *integral insight*, see Schilpp, ed., pp. 60-62.

35. IVL, 138.

36. RRCP, 102.

philosophy and poetry, Radhakrishnan asserts that "the true philosopher with the true poet follows the intuitive method."[37] There are many illustrations throughout Radhakrishnan's writings which illustrate his intuitive method. Early in his career he exclaimed : "In a final intuition we can realize the immediate fact that all is one."[38] For him, integral insight is insight into the alleged oneness of all. In short, Radhakrishnan holds intuition to be *the* source of certitude. For instance, he claims that "Intuitive truths as simple acts of mental vision are free from doubt."[39] His intuitive method requires one to seize the real in a direct act.[40] He explains that Indian thought requires us "to surrender to the deepest self where we get into immediate contact with reality."[41] Radhakrishnan says intuitive knowledge or integral insight is "knowledge of immediate apprehension of reality."[42] He contends that knowledge of God is "Unmediated apprehension of the primordial Spirit."[43] These are just a few of the passages which describe Radhakrishnan's intuitive method. They illustrate his idea that the one (also called the Real, the primordial Spirit, the deepest Self) presents itself with immediacy.

The third background concept in the philosophy professor's epistemology is that truth has many sides. He explains :

> From the beginning the Indian felt that truth was many-sided, and different views contained different aspects of truth which no one could fully express... Of course there are dangers incident to such a breadth of view. Often it has led the Indian thinkers into misty vagueness, lazy acceptance and cheap eclecticism.[44]

Clearly, Radhakrishnan is aware of the potential dangers in viewing truth as many-sided. His warning against "lazy accept-

37. PRT, 164. Cf. "facts are apprehended by intuition, whether perceptual or non-perceptual" (PU, 99) and "intuitive consciousness apprehends real things which are not open to the senses" (IVL, 143).
38. "The VP and the DM," 443.
39. IVL, 146.
40. Ibid., 149.
41. S. Radhakrishnan and J. H. Muirhead, eds., CIP, 270.
42. "The VP and the DM," 443.
43. Schilpp, ed., 61.
44. IP, I, 49.

ance" is intended to encourage Indians and others to sift traditions vigorously in order to eliminate some "sides" of traditional truth. The many-sidedness of truth is an important background concept for the study of Jainism as well as Hinduism. As Radhakrishnan puts it :

> *Anekānta-vāda* refers to the richness of reality and the relativity of human conceptions of it. To the Hindu as to the Jaina, truth presents itself in many ways. Each *darśana* is a vision and not complete truth...Reality is complex and to be known should be viewed from many aspects.[45]

Radhakrishnan endorses *anekāntavāda* elsewhere.[46] It is a Sanskrit compound meaning "the way (*vāda*) of final (*anta*) not (*an*) oneness (*eka*)."[47] Radhakrishnan refers to *anekāntavāda* as "the doctrine of the manyness of reality."[48] Radhakrishnan contends that since truth has many sides, there are many paths to truth, many methods for ascertaining truth. Incidentally, an important variation on the theme of truth with many sides is Radhakrishnan's contention that truth has just two sides. He takes the position that there is human truth and absolute truth.[49] We have already seen that he uses at least nine adjectives to describe reality which is not absolute. He also uses these nine adjectives to describe truth which is "human," not absolute. It is not entirely clear why Radhakrishnan claims so often that truth has just two sides.

Fourth and finally, the reader's attention is invited to some criteria for truth, the most important elements in any epistemology. They are the tests and standards used to judge what is the nature of the case. In a chapter criticizing William James, Radhakrishnan rejects the pragmatist's criterion for truth : "There is all the difference in the world between 'It is useful

45. OSW, 1952-1959, 369.

46. Ibid., 302. Cf. "The teaching of the *Gītā*...is articulated by a profound seer who sees truth in its many-sidedness" (BG, 12).

47. Our translation.

48. IP, I, 304. Karl H. Potter says it means "the view that ultimates are not single," in *Presuppositions of India's Philosophies* (Englewood Cliffs, New Jersey: Prentice-Hall, 1963), p. 114.

49. RRCP, 234.

because it is true' and 'It is true because it is useful'."[50] Throughout his writings, Radhakrishnan accepts numerous other criteria for knowing the truth : (1) three criteria stated in *An Idealist View of Life*; (2) coherence; (3) persistence, permanence, and immutability; (4) distance from the absolute; (5) deepest convictions; and (6) self-evidence.

In a brief section of *An Idealist View of Life* entitled "Belief and Certainty," Radha krishnan states three epistemological criteria: "We reach absolute logical certainty, if what we find to be true is supported by others, if it is coherent with knowledge and works in life."[51] His criterion "works in life" is at best confusing and at worst equivocal. The pragmatic criterion *usefulness* cannot be true for Radhakrishnan and false for William James. The criterion "supported by others" parallels "scriptural testimony," one of the four classical means of knowledge (*pramāṇas*) in Indian thought. They are : (1) perception; (2) inference; (3) scriptural testimony; and (4) analogy. Generally, Radhakrishnan seldom refers to these four *pramāṇas* in discussions of epistemological method. He is critical of what he calls Nyāya's pre-occupation with logic and method.

Radhakrishnan often uses coherence as the test for truth. He states : "In philosophical interpretation, the most coherent view is the most true."[52] Referring pejoratively to the correspondence "notion," Radhakrishnan indicates that "The Nyāya, in spite of its allegiance to the correspondence notion, grasps the more adequate character of the coherence theory."[53] In a discussion which minimizes the significance of perception, he proclaims that "Even where complete perceptual verification is out of the question, we may apply the criterion of coherence."[54] Elsewhere[55] he substitutes coherence and inclusiveness for correspondence as the test of truth. Western thinkers usually do not associate *inclusiveness* with coherence. To be true, Radhakrishnan reasons, a proposition must be inclusive—it must cohere

50. RRCP, 244.
51. IVL, 222.
52. IP, I, 674.
53. IP, II, 138.
54. RRCP, 246.
55. IVL, 169.

with the *whole* of reality. He writes: "Coherence not with this or that aspect but with the whole of experience is the essence of truth."[56] Coherence for Radhakrishnan refers to something more than the cohering of abstract propositions in a formal system. It refers to cohering of an ontological sort.

Persistence, permanence, and immutability are important criteria for truth in Radhakrishnan and *advaita vedānta* philosophy. For instance, Radhakrishnan writes: "If persistence or permanence is supposed to be the test of reality, we find it is only the whole that is real, for only that is unchanging while the finite changes."[57] Another contemporary *Vedāntin*, S. O. Ramakrishnan, writes: " 'Persistence' or 'Unsublatability' (abādita [*sic*]) is the criterion of Truth and Reality in Advaita."[58] Incidentally, this passage illustrates the epistemological confusion surrounding the translation of *sat* and *satya* as "reality" and "truth" respectively. Sanskrit *sat* and *satya* are closer to each other etymologically than English *reality* and *truth.* Indian philosophy identifies truth and reality (e.g., *satya* in Gandhi's thought). In Western thinking, truth refers to the nature of a judgment whereas reality refers to the nature of the case. Many passages in Radhakrishnan's writings contain variations on the theme of persistence, permanence, and immutability as criteria for truth : "The test of reality is......persistence for all time";[59] "If immutability is the criterion of reality";[60] "If the constant is the real";[61] and "Whatever is limited or transitory is not real."[62] Radhakrishnan's two levels of truth, human and absolute, are reflected in permanence as a criterion for truth. Permanence is absolutely true and real; flux is not absolutely true or real. In so far as *māyā* has ontological meaning, it signifies flux not permanence.

56. RRCP, 245.

57. "The VP and the DM," 440.

58. "The Doctrine of Maya," *The Vedanta Kesari* 49 (June 1962): 110. Ramakrishnan's *abādita* should read *abādhita* from $\sqrt{}$*bādh*, "to press hard; distress; beset" (C. R. Lanman, *A Sanskrit Reader* [Cambridge: Harvard University Press, 1967], s.v. "$\sqrt{}$*bādh*"). Radhakrishnan translates *a-bādhita* as "non-contradiction" (HPEW, I, 279).

59. IP, II, 458.

60. PU, 86.

61. BS, 136.

62. IP, I, 534.

Distance from the absolute is used by Radhakrishnan to determine degree of reality. For instance, he claims that "we are able to ascertain the degrees of reality possessed by the objects of the world by measuring the distance separating them from the One."[63] He states this criterion elsewhere.[64] Without a clear and distinct idea of an absolute, it is difficult to understand this epistemological criterion. However, if we assume with Radhakrishnan an ontological absolute, we can measure the distance between that absolute and the objects of the world. Degrees of reality are then simply a matter of yards or metres. If Radhakrishnan means "measure" in another way, he never says how.

Deepest convictions as a criterion for truth might be expected from someone like Radhakrishnan who relies heavily upon an intuitive epistemology. He judges that "our deepest convictions give us trustworthy knowledge of ultimate reality, perhaps the only knowledge possible."[65] Scriptures record the deepest convictions of the early rishis and prophets. This criterion for truth parallels the classical *pramāṇa* scriptural testimony. Sounding like Paul Tillich, Radhakrishnan writes : "Truth is that which reveals itself to those who have sounded the depths of experience."[66] The problem with using deepest convictions as a criterion for truth is that frequently two people have equally deep convictions that their mutually contradictory judgments are true.

Finally, Radhakrishnan appeals to self-evidence as an epistemological criterion. He claims that "Pure being is self-evidencing (*svayaṁprakāśa*)."[67] Elsewhere Radhakrishnan writes : "That something is real is a self-evident truth, and it is its nature that we have to understand."[68] Were the truth of something as self-evident as Radhakrishnan claims, equally intelligent, sincere, and pious people would never disagree. The weakness of self-

63. IP, I, 168.
64. See IP, I, 184; IP, I, 199; PU, 85.
65. IVL, 220.
66. IP, II, 140.
67. HPEW, I, 278. See IP, II, 500: "Cognitions are said to be self-luminous (*svapràkāśa*)." *svaprakāśa* is from $\sqrt{}$*kās* + *sva*. $\sqrt{}$*kās* means "be visible; shine." *sva* means "own." The root plus prefix means "shine out; become clear."
68. IP, I, 199. On "self-evidence," see J. G. Arapura, *Radhakrishnan and Integral Experience*, p. 106.

evidence as a criterion for truth is readily apparent. For instance, I could claim that self-evidence as an epistemological criterion is invalid. Then I could support my claim by saying that it is self-evident.

To summarize Radhakrishnan's epistemological background concepts, he thinks reality in its wholeness cannot be grasped by the discursive intellect. He views knowledge as intuitive and calls it integral insight. Intuitive knowledge is gained in a mode of presentational immediacy. Radhakrishnan thinks that truth is many-sided; he often states that truth has just two levels. His criteria for truth are : coherence; persistence, permanence, and immutability; distance from the absolute; deepest convictions; and self-evidence. We move now to a discussion of ontological background concepts in Radhakrishnan's philosophy.

III. Ontological Concepts

This section identifies six background concepts which express what Radhakrishnan asserts to be the nature of the case : (1) reality; (2) unity and continuity; (3) consciousness; (4) the whole; (5) harmony; and (6) truth.

Radhakrishnan's ontology raises a crucial question regarding the nature of reality: Is reality growing ? In different passages Radhakrishnan answers this question both ways. On the one hand, he often cites with approval Śaṅkara's position that "the real must be exempt from all change and persist for all time"[69] and "The real is that which persists for all time."[70] In other words, Śaṅkara's position is that reality is changeless, eternally persistent and therefore not subject to growth. This ontological view is consistent with *advaita vedānta* epistemology in which persistence, permanence, and immutability are criteria for truth. On the other hand, Radhakrishnan's etymology of *Brahman*, the theological parallel for reality, suggests that reality grows, expands, and evolves. Radhakrishnan reports :

> The Upaniṣads raise the question; [*sic*] what is that reality which remains identical and persists through change ?

69. HVL, 46.
70. Brightman, ed., *Proceedings*, 685.

> The word used in the Upaniṣads to indicate the supreme reality is *brahman*. It is derived from the root *bṛh*, 'to grow, to burst forth.' The derivation suggests gushing forth, bubbling over, ceaseless growth, *bṛhattvam*. Śaṁkara derives the word '*brahman*' from the root *bṛhati* to exceed, *atiśayana* [*sic*] and means by it eternity, purity.[71]

Radhakrishnan states in a matter-of-fact manner that his etymology differs from Śaṅkara's. Elsewhere Radhakrishnan writes : "The word Brahman...is derived from the root *brih-* to grow."[72] He ends another discussion of the word *brahman* : "To us, it is clear, Brahman means reality, which grows, breathes, or swells."[73] In short, Radhakrishnan's etymology suggests that Brahman means growth. Paradoxically, he says reality is changeless, eternally persistent, on the one hand, and growing, on the other.

No background concept is more central to Radhakrishnan's ontology than unity. He is thoroughly convinced that unity is ultimately the nature of the case. The intensity of his conviction is evident in thirteen passages written during all periods of his life :

(1) Indian people...were more intent on seeking the unity of things than emphasizing their sharpness and separation;
(2) Philosophy bade men seek beneath all change, which is the law of life, unity and persistency;
(3) We have also the conviction of the unity of the universe;
(4) The unity of all life, which is the intellectual assumption of science, becomes the consuming conviction of the sage;
(5) If we are impressed by one thing more than another, it is the oneness of nature and the fundamental unity of origin of all classes of 'atoms';
(6) Though the world is always changing, it has a unity and a meaning;
(7) Where there is the spirit of the Lord, there is unity;
(8) oneness of things is the pivotal principle of absolutism;
(9) The *Advaita Vedānta* emphasizes the unity of being, the oneness of the subject;

71. PU, 52.
72. RRCP, 443.
73. IP, I, 164, fn. 1.

(10) The first principle of the universe possesses unity;
(11) Unity...is the necessary result of the interaction of subjects who are all guided by the same impulse;
(12) All life is a unity and the unity is derived from the initial impetus;
(13) The insistence on the unity of the Supreme Self as the constitutive reality of the world and of the individual souls does not negate the empirical reality of the latter.[74]

These statements about unity are neither verifiable nor falsifiable. They are confessional in nature. Other passages which assume or confess unity raise three related new issues.

First, unity is not oneness for Radhakrishnan. In this respect, his monism is more defensible than most. He explains that "the unity is not one which annuls the distinctions but one which includes them all."[75] Elsewhere he specifies that "Uniformity is not the meaning of unity."[76] It is incorrect, says Radhakrishnan, to "reduce unity to identity."[77] He expresses paradoxically that the Absolute is "an eternal unity involving differentiations."[78] Radhakrishnan has a virtually unlimited reservoir of phrases for saying the same things in slightly different ways. He speaks of making the absolute "a unity with a difference."[79] Elsewhere he decrees : "What is, is an identity in difference."[80] Most germane to our overall project on *māyā* is the following :

> While a few Hindus insist on ultimate unity to the extent of rejecting diversity as illusion and renouncing all action, all desire, all that is corporeal, the majority of the Hindus look upon the unity as reality itself in diversity of creation and demanding devotion and love from the creatures.[81]

74. (1) IP, I, 30; (2) "The VP and the DM," 433; (3) IVL, 109; (4) ERWT, 52; (5) IP, II, 240; (6) ERWT, 89; (7) RF, 198; (8) RRCP, 234; (9) BS, 140; (10) IVL, 332; (11) RRCP, 131; (12) RRCP, 150; (13) PU, 93-94.

75. RRCP, 139.

76. HVL, 69.

77. RRCP, 417.

78. "The VP and the DM," 451. Cf. "We have of course degrees of oneness" (IP, II, 245).

79. IP, I, 185. Cf. "The Vedānta Sūtras declare that the Brahman is a unity in variety and not a pure blank identity." ("The VP and the DM," 446)

80. RRCP, 198.

81. PCF, 22.

Radhakrishnan dissociates himself from those allegedly "few Hindus" who insist on rejecting diversity as illusion. He accepts some meanings of *māyā*, but he rejects the meaning *illusion*. In short, Radhakrishnan's unity manifests diversity. Paradoxically, his "one" is not singular.

Second, Radhakrishnan's unity raises the issue of external relations. He definitely thinks "The conception of a plurality of reals externally related to one another must yield place to the idea of the essential unity of the world."[82] He objects to the absolute independence of relata. We shall see that *māyā*[6] means one-sided dependence. In Radhakrishnan's mind, *māyā*[6] eliminates the possibility of a mutual, two-sided dependency between the one and the many.[83]

Third, Radhakrishnan's unity implies that the world is getting better and better. He posits an "impulse towards union and co-operation which is a fact of history."[84] He claims there is "growing unification, the impulse toward unity."[85] He thinks things are getting better and better in the relations among world religions. This is due to an alleged "transcendent unity of religions which is above their empirical diversity."[86] In this, one can only hope that Radhakrishnan is correct.

Continuity and unity are closely related background concepts in Radhakrishnan's thought. In the last chapter of *An Idealist View of Life*, he differentiates six pervasive characteristics of the world : "First, it is an ordered whole. We find an unbroken continuity, a complete unity from the changes in the atoms to the movements of history."[87] Radhakrishnan views the world as a whole which displays continuity and unity at all levels. Radhakrishnan's continuity seems to be the temporal aspect of his a-temporal unity. Discussing rebirth, he argues that "The way of nature is continuity within a certain general pattern. If the general plan of consecutiveness is not to be violated, the

82. IP, II, 140.
83. RRCP, 339.
84. RRCP, 132.
85. RRCP, 276.
86. RF, 188.
87. IVL, 312. Cf. "Intuition assumes the continuity and unity of all experience" (Ferm, ed., 38).

human selves must continue after death."[88] It is clear from this statement and its context that Radhakrishnan sees a close relationship between continuity and *karma-saṃsāra*. An interesting experiment would be to substitute *karma-saṃsāra* for continuity and observe whether Radhakrishnan's meaning changes. In an interesting rebuttal of the common objection that the theory of rebirth is untrue because memory of past lives is lacking, Radhakrishnan claims that "The metaphysical question of the continuity of the self is not in any way affected by the discontinuity of memory."[89] Regardless of the validity of this rebuttal, clearly continuity is an important background concept in Radhakrishnan's ontology.

Consciousness is as important as unity in Radhakrishnan's thought. *Indian Philosophy*, volume two, contains eight passages which illustrate his view of consciousness :

(1) reality in itself, on which our theory of knowledge should take its stand, the primary ontological fact, is consciousness (caitanya);
(2) The only absolute, then, is the undivided reality of consciousness;
(3) Unless we assume the reality of self as consciousness, the explanation of consciousness becomes difficult;
(4) The basis of all is consciousness and not externality;
(5) The fundamental fact of a universal consciousness is the presupposition of all knowledge;
(6) Consciousness has no limit, since the consciousness of limits shows that the consciousness is greater than the limit;
(7) Consciousness must be assumed as the primal fact;
(8) there is only caitanya, or pure consciousness.[90]

The references to *caitanya*, pure consciousness, make one wonder if F. S. C. Northrop's "Undifferentiated aesthetic continuum" is taken directly from the concept "undivided caitanya." Other

88. IVL, 288. Cf. Radhakrishnan's warning against a "breach in the law of continuity" (RRCP, 87).

89. IVL, 299. Cf. "Karma is not so much a principle of retribution as one of continuity" (IVL, 275).

90. These eight passages are found on the following pages of IP, II: (1) 138; (2) 138; (3) 154; (4) 244; (5) 306; (6) 483-484; (7) 493; (8) 575.

passages raise other issues. For instance, Radhakrishnan uses this background concept to avoid solipsism : "Idealistic monism gets over this difficulty [solipsism] by positing a universal consciousness which includes the individual consciousnesses and serves as a bond of union and basis of agreement."[91] How are persons and animals different ? Radhakrishnan answers : "Consciousness and choice distinguish men from other species."[92] Another passage raises several issues :

> Consciousness cannot be defined. It is awareness of thinking, imagining, sensing. There are four states of consciousness according to the *Māṇḍūkya* U., waking, dream and sleep, and the transcendental consciousness called *turīya*.[93]

First, the fact that Radhakrishnan says consciousness cannot be defined and then defines it indicates that we are dealing with a particularly significant and paradoxical concept. Second, consciousness is conceived as having four states. We shall see how Radhakrishnan related *Māṇḍūkya Upaniṣad's* four states of consciousness to his own vision of reality with four poises.

The whole is an important ontological concept in Radhakrishnan's writings before 1932. Just as unity and consciousness have been portrayed by lists of Radhakrishnan's own words, so is his concept of the whole :

(1) Reality is the whole, and it is one system;
(2) The true is the whole, and the untrue is the fragmentary or the limited;
(3) the one whole is the metaphysical ultimate;
(4) The whole is the explanation of all its parts or stages. It alone is ultimately real while all else has a dependent and derivative reality;
(5) philosophy simply points out the logical necessity of a whole;
(6) The ultimate reality is that in which we live, move and have our being. It is the whole or the totality;
(7) The Absolute is an organised whole, with interrelated

91. RRCP, 276.
92. RF, 92.
93. BS, 145.

parts in it...The whole has existence through the parts, and the parts are intelligible only through the whole;

(8) Diversity, distinction and plurality have a meaning only within a whole.[94]

Unity, consciousness, and the whole are non-theological terms for Brahman. In *An Idealist View of Life* Radhakrishnan touches on *Gestalt-theorie* and develops a view of the self (Ātman) as an organized whole.[95] The young Radhakrishnan found in F. H. Bradley an absolutist whose views parallel the views of *advaita vedānta.* He uses Bradley to explain *advaita vedānta* to the West. For instance, Bradley writes :

> We have found that no one aspect of experience, as such, is real. None is primary, or can serve to explain the others or the whole. They are all alike appearances, all one-sided, and passing away beyond themselves.[96]

Radhakrishnan often uses these identical words. His *parts* cannot explain the whole. They are *passing away*. They are *appearances* in the sense of *vivarta*, though not in the sense of illusion. They are *one-sided*, dependent on the whole (this is the meaning of *māyā*[6]). Describing the relation between Brahman and the world as a relation between the whole and its parts enabled the early Radhakrishnan to affirm the reality of both unity and diversity, both whole and parts, both Brahman and the world. Radhakrishnan's early arguments against an illusional interpretation of *māyā* rely heavily upon this whole-parts theme.

Another background concept in Radhakrishnan's philosophy is harmony. He claims : "The harmony of the world is neither pre-established nor externally imposed. It is the nature of things."[97] Elsewhere Radhakrishnan exhorts : "In the art of life Tagore wishes us to practise the synoptic vision of the harmony of the whole and wholeness of personality, not antagonism between parts."[98] The lack of harmony among parts was a source

94. (1) "The VP and the DM," 439; (2) Ibid., 440; (3) RRCP, 59; (4) RRCP, 85; (5) RRCP, 207; (6) RRCP, 414; (7) RRCP, 443; (8) IP, II, 230.

95. IVL, p. 264, pp. 266-269.

96. F. H. Bradley, *Appearance and Reality*, 2d ed. (Oxford: The Clarendon Press, 1897; Oxford University Press paperback, 1969), p. 429.

97. RRCP, 88.

98. PRT, 221.

of pain and disappointment to Radhakrishnan, especially later in life while he was in public office. In his later writings, Radhakrishnan places great value on *samavāya* (concord). For instance, he instructs: "Concord, not discord, will contribute to the establishment of spiritual values in the life of mankind. Concord alone is meritorious, said Aśoka : *Samavāya eva sādhuḥ.*"[99] Harmony and concord are not unrelated to unity and the whole. To establish harmony and unity, especially in the intellectual realm, was Radhakrishnan's purpose in life. He had an uncanny ability to combine points of view. For instance, he tries to see harmony among Hegel, Marx, and himself :

> The truth in the doctrine of the dialectical movement of history is that from the conflict of contradictory opinions and interests, and from their discussion, new knowledge in the theoretical sphere and new institutions in the practical world arise; for all nature seeks a harmony and cannot rest content with an unsolved discord.[100]

Hegelian theory and Marxist praxis are supposedly harmonized in typically Radhakrishnanian fashion. We have seen how Radhakrishnan's idealism is teleological. Ideas and values are operative creative forces which drive the universe in a meaningful direction. They draw the world from what it is to what it should be. Harmony is an outstanding example of such a teleological idea or value.

Finally, Radhakrishnan's ontology identifies reality and truth. He writes :

> For in intuition the knower plunges into the flux of reality and knows that reality from within by being one with it. It is knowledge that swims within the stream of life. Here truth is completely identified with reality.[101]

This identification of reality and truth helps explain why Radhakrishnan and other Indian thinkers are not bothered when *sat* and *satya* are translated *reality* and *truth.* The identification of truth

99. OSW, 1952-1959, 337.

100. RS, 34-35.

101. RRCP, 189. Cf. "Truth in spiritual life is neither the reflection nor the expression of any other reality. It is reality itself." (PU, 98).

and reality is a recurring theme in Gandhi's thought. Discussing *satyāgraha*, Radhakrishnan quotes Gandhi as follows :

> The world rests on the bedrock of satya or truth. Asatya, meaning untruth, also means non-existent, and satya, or truth, means 'that which is.' If untruth does not so much as exist, its victory is out of the question. And truth being 'that which is' can never be destroyed.[102]

In short, truth is real and untruth is unreal. It may not be an overstatement to say that nothing in the Hindu tradition was more responsible for Gandhi's success than this conviction that truth is reality. Referring to some of Gandhi's statements ("Truth is that which *is*; error that which *is not.*" and "Truth is God."), J. H. Muirhead reports : "It seemed worthwhile to experiment by substituting in all such passages 'reality' for 'truth' and noting how far this would clarify the situation."[103] Muirhead's substitution clarified very little. The power of truth to change ontological reality is discussed by Heinrich Zimmer. Recounting several tales from Hindu lore, Zimmer explains that in Hindu tradition "a heartfelt truth of any order has its force. Even a shameful truth is better than a decent falsehood."[104] To what degree Radhakrishnan shares Gandhi's belief in the formative power of truth would be an interesting question to pursue. The point here is that reality/truth is an ontological background concept in Radhakrishnan's philosophy.

To summarize Radhakrishnan's ontological concepts, he views reality as changeless but paradoxically gives an etymology of the parallel concept Brahman which suggests growth, expansion, and evolution. He is convinced that the universe is a unity. Paradoxically, his "one" is not singular. Continuity is a closely related concept, the temporal aspect of his a-temporal unity and closely related to *karma-saṃsāra*. Consciousness is undivided, internal, pure, not definable and yet it has four states. The whole

102. S. Radhakrishnan, ed., MG, 31.

103. J. H. Muirhead, "The Hindu Idea of Truth," in S. Radhakrishnan, ed., MG, 381.

104. Heinrich Zimmer, *Philosophies of India* (Princeton, New Jersey: Princeton University Press, 1951), p. 167. Cf. Eugene Watson Burlingame, "The Act of Truth (Saccakiriya): A Hindu Spell and its Employment as a Psychic Motif in Hindu Fiction," *Journal of the Royal Asiatic Society* (1917): 429-467.

and its parts are both real although the dependency is one-sided. Harmony and concord are ontological and teleological. Finally, truth is completely identified with reality.

IV. The Concept of Reality in Four Poises

This section presents evidence to support the judgment that no concept in Radhakrishnan's mature hermeneutics is more important than the background concept of reality in four poises. Examined here are : (1) statements of reality in four poises; (2) Brahman and *Īśvara* as recurring polarities; (3) *Hiraṇyagarbha*; and (4) *Virāṭ*.

Radhakrishnan's statements of reality in four poises use both Sanskrit and English. Even though he does not develop this concept until his "Introduction" to *The Principal Upaniṣads* (1953), he mentions it earlier in a five-page section entitled "Brahman and Ātman" in *Indian Philosophy*, volume one (1923):

The following table suggests the scheme :

	Subject (Ātman)		*Object (Brahman)*
1.	The bodily self (Viśva).	1.	Cosmos (Virāṭ or Vaiśvānara)
2.	The Vital self (Taijasa).	2.	The soul of the world (Hiraṇyagarbha).
3.	The intellectual self (Prājña).	3.	Self-consciousness (Īśvara)
4.	The intuitive self (Turīya).	4.	Ānanda (Brahman).[105]

These four poises of Ātman are the four states of consciousness suggested in the *Māṇḍūkya Upaniṣad.* Radhakrishnan affirms the identity of Ātman and Brahman (*tattvamasi*). He then develops the four poises of reality so that they will express objectively what the *Māṇḍūkya Upaniṣad's* four poises of Ātman express subjectively.

In his "Introduction" to his translation of *The Principal Upaniṣads*, Radhakrishnan spells out in great detail his concept of reality in four poises :

105. IP, I, 172.

> We thus get the four poises or statuses of reality, the Absolute, *Brahman*, (2) the Creative Spirit, *Īśvara*, (3) the World-Spirit, *Hiraṇya-garbha*, and (4) the World. This is the way in which the Hindu thinkers interpret the integral nature of the Supreme Reality. *Māṇḍūkya Upaniṣad* says that Brahman is *catuṣ-pāt*, four-footed, and its four principles are *Brahman*, *Īśvara*, *Hiraṇya-garbha* and *Virāj*.[106]

The etymological derivations of the Sanskrit names for the four poises help very little to explain the layers of meaning which Radhakrishnan attaches to each name. We have seen that Radhakrishnan derives *Brahman* from $\sqrt{}$*bṛh* meaning "to grow." *Īśvara* derives from $\sqrt{}$*iś* meaning "to be master of." *Hiraṇya-garbha* is a compound comprised of *hiraṇya* ("gold") and *garbha* ("womb") which means "the golden womb." Radhakrishnan uses *Hiraṇyagarbha* and Brahmā interchangeably. *Virāṭ* derives from $\sqrt{}$*rāj*+*vi* meaning "ruling far and wide, sovereign."[107] Radhakrishnan uses *Virāṭ* to signify "world, cosmos. "These Sanskrit names for the four poises of reality appear frequently.[108]

Other passages use English names for the four poises of reality. For instance, Radhakrishnan claims that :

> The *Ṛg Veda* is familiar with the four-fold distinction of (i) the Absolute, the One, beyond all dualities and distinctions, (ii) the self-conscious Subject confronting the object, (iii) the World-soul, and (iv) the world.[109]

As Radhakrishnan develops his concept of reality in four poises, a pattern begins to emerge which is important in his interpretation of *māyā*. The fourth poise of reality, *Virāṭ*, is the world. The four distinctions of reality are used in order to show that the world is quite real. It has value and meaning just as the other three poises have value and meaning. Radhakrishnan explains :

> We have thus the four sides of one whole : (i) the tran-

106. PU, 65.

107. These meanings are given in Monier Monier-Williams, *A Sanskrit-English Dictionary* under their respective roots.

108. See ERWT, 127; PU, 66; PU, 76; PU, 90; PU, 701-705; BS, 118-135; BS, 143; BS, 207; Schilpp, ed., 41; and OSW, 1952-1959, 321; *Encyclopedia Britannica*, 14th ed., s.v. "Indian Philosophy."

109. PU, 39-40.

> scendental universal being anterior to any concrete reality; (ii) the causal principle of all differentiation; (iii) the innermost essence of the world; and (iv) the manifest world. They are co-existent and not alternating poises where we have either a quiescent *Brahman* or a creative Lord. These are simultaneous sides of the one Reality.[110]

He is careful to point out that the real is not the sum of four parts but "an ineffable unity in which these conceptual distinctions are made."[111] He warns that to identify the real with any one poise is to violate the unity and divide the indivisible.[112] The importance of the background concept *unity* is evident. Radhakrishnan's writings contain other English explanations of his concept of reality in four poises.[113] The most important passage for our study of *māyā* is his admonition : "If we keep in mind the fourfold character of the Supreme, we shall avoid confusion in regard to the status of the world."[114] Confusion will be avoided because the world will be seen as an integral part of the scheme of things entire. It will be seen as a part which has meaning and value.

Brahman and *Īśvara* are poise one and poise two, respectively. The polarity between Brahman and *Īśvara* parallels three other polarities: Absolute and God, the transpersonal and the personal, and *nirguṇa* Brahman and *saguṇa* Brahman. Generally, these polarities between poises one and two are the most important concepts in Radhakrishnan's understanding of reality. He says "there are many analogies to the conception of *Brahman* and *Īśvara*, Absolute and God in Western religious thought."[115] Radhakrishnan is particularly fond of quoting Meister Eckhart's distinction between Godhead and God. Poise one and poise two, says Radhakrishnan, are distinctions of logic not ontology. To understand him at this point, we must keep in mind his many-sided view of reality. He writes : "*Brahman* and *Īśvara* are not

110. PU, 92.

111. PU, 66.

112. Ibid.

113. See PU, 63; PU, 122; PU, 126; PU, 143; PU, 705. Cf. also Schilpp, ed., 64, 797; EW, 57.

114. PU, 90. The complete paragraph containing this sentence is cited below in Chapter three, Section three.

115. BS, 131.

distinct entities but different aspects of the same Reality."[116] He explains that "the distinction is only logical."[117] Radhakrishnan's concept of reality in four poises gives no ontological priority to Brahman. He declares :

> The tendency to regard *Īśvara* or God as phenomenal and Brahman or the Absolute as real is not correct. This is a distinction of great significance which we should preserve, if we are to have a balanced view of the Supreme. Professor Brightman's whole criticism about my vacillation between the non-dualism of Śaṁkara and the personal theism of Rāmānuja is based on the postulate that the Supreme must be either the one or the other, which I do not admit.[118]

Radhakrishnan's affirmation of both poise one and poise two rejects the either-or way of thinking. His concept of reality in four poises uses both-and thinking. *Both* poise one *and* poise two are equally real. Radhakrishnan's four-poises conception seems to be a deliberate attempt to unite the views of Śaṅkara and Rāmānuja. Neither Śaṅkara's Absolute nor Rāmānuja's personal God is more significant than the other in Radhakrishnan's philosophical vision. This point becomes important for understanding his *māyā* hermeneutics when we consider poise four, the world. The logical implication of the fourfold concept of reality is that the world and the other three poises are of equal ontological significance, even though poise one is logically prior to the other three.

The Absolute and God parallel Brahman and *Iśvara*, poise one and poise two. Radhakrishnan reports that:

> According to the Upaniṣads, the Absolute and God are one; we call it the supreme Brahman to emphasise its transcendence of the finite, its unknowability, its all-comprehensiveness; we call it Īśvara to emphasise the personal aspect so necessary for religious devotion.[119]

We have seen that Radhakrishnan feels deeply about conceiving

116. BS, 126.

117. Schilpp, ed., 796. Cf. "Both the Absolute and the Personal God are real; only the former is the logical prius of the later." (PU, 79).

118. Schilpp, ed., 797.

119. IP, I, 234.

reality as a unity with distinctions, a whole with parts. Here, poise one and poise two as distinctions or parts are simply matters of emphasis. The difference between poise one and poise two is a difference of standpoint. *An Idealist View of Life* ends with : "The Absolute is the precosmic nature of God, and God is the Absolute from the cosmic point of view."[120] The Jainas call these viewpoints or standpoints *nayas*. Elsewhere Radhakrishnan writes : "It is not a question of either an Absolute with an apparent multiplicity or a living God working in this pluralistic universe. The Supreme is both this and that."[121] Here again, Radhakrishnan's both-and way of thinking is evident, a way which contrasts sharply with Aristotelian either-or thinking. Poise one does not exclude poise two. Responding to his critics, Radhakrishnan writes :

> *God and the Absolute.* Professors Hartshorne and Clement Webb raise the question of the relation of God and the Absolute. These are not to be regarded as exclusive of each other. The Supreme in its non-relational aspect is the Absolute; in its active aspect it is God...The abstract possibility and the concrete realisation are both contained in the one reality, which is Absolute-God.[122]

The non-exclusiveness of poises one and two logically extends to poises three and four. Therefore, poise four, the world, and poise one, the Absolute, do not exclude each other. Using this reasoning, Radhakrishnan argues against illusional hermeneutics and for the reality of poise four, the world.

Radhakrishnan views poises one and two as the transpersonal and personal aspects of the Supreme, respectively. In his 1961 lecture, "Fellowship of the Spirit," delivered at the opening of The Center for the Study of World Religions at The Harvard Divinity School, Radhakrishnan cites Rāmakrishna :

> When I think of the Supreme Being as inactive, neither creating, nor preserving nor destroying, I call him *Brahman* or *Puruṣa*, the superpersonal God. When I think of him as active, creating, preserving, destroying, I call him *Śakti* or

120. IVL, 345. Cf. ERWT, 92.
121. BG, 38.
122. Schilpp, ed. 796.

> *māyā* or *prakṛti*, the personal God. But the distinction between them does not mean a difference. The personal and the super-personal are the same Being...[123]

This statement by Rāmakrishna expresses the distinction between poises one and two, a distinction between the transpersonal and the personal. Radhakrishnan claims that "The super-personal and personal aspects of the Supreme may be distinguished in thought but cannot be separated in fact."[124] Elsewhere he explains that :

> In religious experience personal encounter is as real as the encounter of subject and object in cognitive experience. We meet a 'Thou' whom we can influence by prayer and worship. While *Brahman* is the trans-personal ground and abyss of everything personal, *Īśvara* is the Personal God.[125]

Clearly, Radhakrishnan sees the transpersonal and the personal, the Absolute and God, and Brahman and *Īśvara* as parallels.

Nirguṇa Brahman and *saguṇa* Brahman also parallel poises one and two of Radhakrishnan's fourfold paradigm. They are important background concepts in Śaṅkara's philosophy. Radhakrishnan declares that "The conceptions of Brahman and Īśvara, Absolute and God, the Nirguṇa and Saguṇa Brahman of Śaṁkara, are not irreconcilable."[126] Radhakrishnan reconciles them the same way he reconciles their parallels. It is interesting to note that there are very few references to *nirguṇa* Brahman and *saguṇa* Brahman in Radhakrishnan's writings other than references in passages describing the history of Indian philosophy.

Hiraṇyagarbha is poise three. In a discussion of the three principle forces connected with creation in Indian mythology, Bosch writes :

> As to the third principle, the origin of life, it will be seen gradually to take on more definite forms after having first been referred to as something altogether obscure.... RV X 82, 5 calls it *garbha*, meaning 'germ', 'embryo' or

123. FS, 21.

124. ERWT, 292. Cf. BG, 24.

125. BS, 126.

126. S. Radhakrishnan, "Hinduism and the West," in L. S. S. O'Malley, ed., *Modern India and the West* (Oxford: The University Press, 1941), p. 340.

> 'womb', and X 121 for the first time use the term Hiraṇya-garbha, 'the golden germ' or 'the golden womb'.[127]

The early Vedic poets used *germ* and *womb* interchangeably. Radhakrishnan pictures *hiraṇya-garbha* as "literally gold-germ, source of golden light, the world-soul, from which all powers and existences of this world are derived. It comes later to mean Brahmā, the creator of the world."[128] He uses *Hiraṇyagarbha* and *Brahmā* interchangeably. Radhakrishnan's most complete exposition of this third poise of reality is in *Indian Philosophy*, volume one, where he sets forth an Upaniṣadic analogy :

> This Hiraṇyagarbha is looked upon as related to the universe in the same way as the individual soul is related to its body.... The world in which we live has its own mind, and this mind is Hiraṇyagarbha. This conception of world soul appears in the Upaniṣads under various names and forms. It is called Kārya Brahma, or the effect God...as distinguished from the Kāraṇa Brahma or the Causal God of Īśvara. ...This effect God is the totality of created existences of which all finite objects are parts.[129]

Generally, *world-soul* or *world-spirit* is the best translation. If the universe is personified as having a body, *Hiraṇyagarbha* is its soul. The title of Radhakrishnan's inaugural address at Oxford University, "The World's Unborn Soul," suggests poise three of his fourfold concept of reality.

Virāṭ is poise four in Radhakrishnan's concept of reality with four poises. He uses *Virāṭ* to signify *world, cosmos.* Radhakrishnan sometimes refers to *Hiraṇyagarbha* and *Virāṭ* as subtle and gross matter, respectively. If poise three is the world-soul, poise four is the world. Radhakrishnan explains :

> When we identify the Ātman with our body, Brahman becomes the Cosmos or the Virāṭ. Virāṭ is the all, the hypostatisation of the conception of the world as a whole. It is the totality of things, the sum of all existence....The body of the Virāṭ is made of the material objects in their aggregate.[130]

127. F. D. K. Bosch, *The Golden Germ : An Introduction to Indian Symbolism* (The Hague, The Netherlands: Mouton and Company, 1960), p. 53.
128. PU, 37, fn. 5.
129. IP, I, 171.
130. Ibid.

In the *Māṇḍūkya Upaniṣad's* fourfold concept of consciousness, *Virāṭ* corresponds with the waking state. In the equation of Brahman and *Ātman*, each with four poises, *Virāṭ* corresponds with the bodily self. In short, poise four is the material universe.

To summarize Radhakrishnan's concept of reality in four poises, the reader's attention has been invited to statements which give the names in both Sanskrit and English. Brahman and *Īśvara* are poise one and poise two. Three parallel polarities have been considered : (1) the Absolute and God; (2) the trans-personal and the personal; and (3) *nirguṇa* Brahman and *saguṇa* Brahman. Poise three of reality is *Hiraṇyagarbha*, the world-soul. Poise four of reality if *Virāṭ*, the world.

3

Recurring Themes in Radhakrishnan's Faith

I. Introduction

This chapter describes S. Radhakrishnan's religious faith, a cornerstone of his *māyā* hermeneutics. His detractors cannot criticize him for having religious faith since it can be shown that all persons have faith of some kind, secular or sacred. On the other hand, the content of Radhakrishnan's faith requires and deserves careful attention from both his proponents and adversaries.

Radhakrishnan's definition of religion is elusive. It is like the *sūtras* in the *Brahma Sūtra* about which he himself asserts : "They refuse, Proteus-like, to be caught in any definite shape."[1] In good Indian fashion Radhakrishnan dislikes what he calls "the Greek spirit" with its "anxiety for definition and form."[2] He declares paradoxically : "The lack of definiteness in a religion like that of the Hindus seems to me to stand for a higher form of definiteness."[3]

After extensive analysis of the term *religion*, Wilfred Cantwell Smith suggests that the question"What is the nature of religion?" be dropped. Instead, he raises questions of "cumulative tradition" and "faith."[4] In keeping with Smith's suggestion, this

1. IP, II, 431.

2. EWR, 49. Cf. "Western forms of religion are inclined to hold that one definition is final and absolute and others are false." (RF, 155).

3. IVL, 204.

4. Wilfred Cantwell Smith, *The Meaning and End of Religion* (New York: New American Library, 1962; a Mentor Books paperback), p. 16, 141.

section describes Radhakrishnan's *faith* rather than his religious *belief*. But what is the nature of *faith*? John A. Hutchison suggests rather convincingly that faith has three aspects :

> Faith (1) may be characterized as the attitude of conviction which organizes and integrates a human self, sets its direction, and determines its action. ...
> Faith (2) consists of particular symbol-systems for the expression and communication of faith (1)...
> Faith (3) is belief, or faith (1) and faith (2) become propositional.[5]

Since Radhakrishnan frequently discusses *religion* and rarely discusses *faith*, this section examines his statements beginning "religion is..." in order to identify his faith (1), faith (2) and faith (3). Generally, Radhakrishnan prefers to discuss faith (1)—his basic attitude of conviction—and to avoid discussing faith (3)—his beliefs. His faith (2)—the symbol-system for expressing and communicating his attitude of conviction—consists of myriad symbols borrowed from the religions of the world. In his attempt to express and communicate an alleged unity of religions, Radhakrishnan melts down their particular symbols and specific beliefs until they express and communicate his own "religion of spirit" which he calls *sanātana dharma*.[6] In the spirit of *Ṛg Veda* I.164.46, he thinks faiths (3) and faiths (2) are many but faith (1) is one.

The reader's attention is invited to seven characteristics of religion as conceived by Radhakrishnan. The philosophy professor describes religion as : (1) an autonomous form of experience; (2) neither dogmatic nor institutional; (3) contact with or insight into reality; (4) personally transforming; (5) born in agony; (6) not a refuge from the world; and (7) feeling which needs an objective philosophy.

In the first place, Radhakrishnan describes religion as an

5. John Alexander Hutchison, "Theology in Global Context," in *Philosophy of Religion and Theology*: 1971, ed. David Griffin (Chambersburg, Pennsylvania: American Academy of Religion, 1971), p. 183.

6. Radhakrishnan's "religion of spirit" is analyzed by Ishwar Chandra Harris, "An Exposition of the Concept of Universalism in Sarvepalli Radhakrishnan's Thought" (Ph.D. dissertation, Claremont, 1974).

autonomous form of experience[7] which invites attention away from the external and towards the internal. Discussing the progress from worship of outer nature which is described in the hymns of the *Ṛg Veda* to the spiritual religion which is described in the Upaniṣads, Radhakrishnan refers to "the law of normal religious growth—man everywhere on earth starts with the external and proceeds to the internal."[8] The attractiveness of Sir Sarvepalli's faith is due in part to this emphasis on inner transformation. However, too much emphasis on the internal has been one of *vedānta's* most questionable legacies. It has developed in conjunction with the illusional interpretation of *māyā* which Radhakrishnan himself tries to eliminate.

Radhakrishnan takes the position that religion is neither dogmatic nor institutional but essentially personal.[9] He feels strongly that dogmas divide whereas religions should unite, that dogmatism is exclusive whereas true religion is inclusive. Dogmas correspond with faith (3), the aspect of faith which Radhakrishnan says he values least. He considers ceremonies to be external forms and insists that religious growth takes place when we look beyond external ceremonies in order to focus on internal experiences.

Thirdly, Radhakrishnan characterizes religion as contact with, or insight into reality :

> Religion is not the acceptance of academic abstractions or the celebration of ceremonies, but a kind of life or experience. It is insight into the nature of reality (*darśana*), or experience of reality (*anubhava*).[10]

Chapter two described Radhakrishnan's philosophical method for acquiring knowledge in a mode of presentational immediacy. His philosophical method and religious approach are quite consistent in this respect. "Religion is, in essence, experience of

7. Ferm, ed., *Religion in Transition*, p. 20.

8. IP, I, 70.

9. RRCP, 283. For the best discussion of this point, see Thomas Paul Urumpackal, *Organized Religion According to Dr. S. Radhakrishnan* (Rome : Universita Gregoriana Editrice, 1972).

10. HVL, 13. Cf. RWN, 27. For discussions of *anubhava* see (1) IP, II, 511 and (2) J. G. Arapura, *Radhakrishnan and Integral Experience* (New York: Asia Publishing House, 1966), pp. 134-135.

or living contact with ultimate reality,"[11] he declares. If mysticism is defined as a philosophical or religious system in which a seeker has immediate apprehension of the sought, then Radhakrishnan is a mystic. He thinks experience of reality (*anubhava*) is experience in which one seizes the real in a direct act. This concept of religion combined with his concept of reality in four poises helps shape his interpretation of *māyā*. For if reality has four poises, contact with it is contact with all four poises. This means that religion is not only a kind of life or experience in which the individual becomes absorbed in Brahman, poise one. Religion must also be a kind of life or experience in which the individual becomes absorbed in poise four, the world.

In the fourth place, Radhakrishnan views religion as personally transforming. "Religion is not so much a theory of the supernatural," he offers, "as an attitude of spirit, a temper of mind."[12] Elsewhere he describes it as "the remaking of your own self, the transformation of your nature."[13] Heinrich Zimmer recalls[14] Srī Rāmakrishna's fable of a tiger cub whose mother died giving birth. The cub was raised by goats until one day a fierce old tiger scared away the goats, leaving the grass-nibbling cub to face danger alone. The old tiger recognized his offspring. He taught the cub to eat red, juicy meat rather than green grass and to roar rather than bleat. Eventually, with a roar of awakening, the tiger cub's nature was transformed. Similarly, Radhakrishnan remarks that "Religion is not for us so much doctrinal conformity or ceremonial piety as the re-changing of our nature, the transforming of our personality—becoming something different from what we are."[15] Streng's definition of religion as "a means of ultimate transformation"[16] comes to mind.

Radhakrishnan's conviction that religion is born in agony challenges the Western stereotype that Eastern spirituality is all

11. Cf. "Religion is not a creed or a code but an insight into reality." (Ferm, ed., *Religion in Transition*, p. 36).

12. Kalki, 47.

13. PRSW, Second Series, 101.

14. See *Philosophies of India* (Princeton, New Jersey: Princeton University Press, 1951), pp. 5-8.

15. PCF, 152.

16. Frederick J. Streng, *Understanding Religious Life*, second edition (Encino, California: Dickenson Publishing Company, 1976), p. 7.

a matter of aesthetic-contemplative, transcendental ecstasy. He told his Oxford audience :

> Religion is born in agony. The one cry of the man who has an apprehension of the Absolute and his own distance from it is that he is a sinner, *pāpo'ham*. When he feels this utter isolation, he is miserable. But this tragedy is also the glory of man.[17]

Tragedy and glory, agony and ecstasy are integral aspects of religious experience. Elsewhere Radhakrishnan describes religion as "the will of the creature to raise himself above himself through toil and effort."[18] In the midst of tragedy and agony, persons strive to transform themselves and their environment. Radhakrishnan thinks "religion is a dynamic process."[19] Elsewhere he proclaims that "Religion is an eternal revolutionary because no order of life can ever satisfy it."[20] Chapter two described Radhakrishnan's idealism in which ideal values have teleological efficacy for guiding the process. They shape the various orders of life through the agonizing toil and effort of religious revolutionaries.

Far from being a refuge from the world, Radhakrishnan argues, religion is "an inspiration to act in the world."[21] His interpretation of *māyā* is intended "to save the world and give to it a real meaning."[22] The attitude of conviction or faith (1) which gives to the world a real meaning also requires responsible action in the world. Conversely, inspiration to act in the world requires an attitude of conviction that the world is meaningful.

Finally, Radhakrishnan thinks religion is feeling which needs an objective philosophy. Against absolute subjectivists he writes: "Religion is a matter of feeling, and for it to be shared with others an objective philosophy is needed. Feeling in and by itself is private and dumb."[23] Background concepts in Radhakrishnan's own "objective philosophy" were identified in chapter two.

17. ERWT, 299-300.
18. RCW, 125.
19. RS, 78.
20. S. Radhakrishnan and J. H. Muirhead, eds., CIP, 288.
21. RCW, 139.
22. See Appendix V.
23. RRCP, 21.

Concepts like unity, continuity, and reality in four poises help him share his faith with others. Without such concepts, religious feelings could never be communicated. In this "Introduction" we have called attention to Radhakrishnan's view of religion in general. Now we are ready to introduce the specific content of his Hindu faith.

II. The Content of S. Radhakrishnan's Faith

This section identifies the content of Sir Sarvepalli's faith (1), faith (2) and faith (3). These three aspects of his faith are separated for purposes of logical analysis, but of course the cannot be reparated in fact. Some passages clearly illustrate one particular aspect of his faith, but most passages contain elements of all three.

Radhakrishnan's faith (1) is his attitude of conviction which organizes and integrates him as a person, sets his direction, and determines his action. It is a tapestry with many colored threads woven into a complex pattern. The tapestry's component parts begin to emerge from Radhakrishnan's best description of his own faith (1):

> There is a mode of consciousness which is distinct from the perceptual, imaginative or intellectual, and this carries with it self-evidence and completeness. Religious men of all ages have won their certainty of God through this direct way of approach to the apprehension of reality.
>
> The larger environment is of the nature of one's own self, with which the individual occasionally comes into contact. There are differences regarding the interpretation of the nature of this spiritual environment, while this at any rate is true, that it offers the only justification for a life of truth seeking and good realising.
>
> The intuition of the all-pervading unity of the self and the universe is emphasised sometimes to the extent of rejecting a God who can reciprocate our love or a self which has real independence.
>
> Those who have this consciousness are the saintly souls whose lives are characterised by an unshakable faith in the supre-

> macy of spirit, invincible optimism, ethical universalism and religious toleration.
>
> The attainment of steady spiritual insight is the aim of religious endeavour and the means to it are an ethical life and the art of meditation."[24]

The first paragraph states in effect that intuitive knowledge is gained in a mode of presentational immediacy. Radhakrishnan proposes that truly religious persons apprehend reality directly. Their apprehension of reality in this mode is said to be self-evident. The second paragraph affirms the identity of the larger environment and one's own true self. This identity gets expressed and communicated by the Hindu symbol *Brahman-Ātman*. As a belief it gets stated in the proposition "That art Thou" (*tat tvam asi*). The third paragraph states that a God who reciprocates love is sometimes unnecessary. Radhakrishnan's attitude of conviction is virtually trans-theistic. Furthermore, his faith (1) virtually eliminates the idea of an independent individual self (*jīva*). Radhakrishnan seems to think that the true self (*Ātman*) is known in the abandonment of a sense of independence, individuality and separateness. The fourth paragraph delineates four specific ideals including optimism and tolerance which operate as creative forces guiding the process of events entire. The final paragraph affirms that salvation (*mokṣa*) is steady insight achieved by both contemplation *and* action.

In the "Conclusion" to *Recovery of Faith* Radhakrishnan gives a name to his own faith :

> The religion outlined in these pages may be called the *sanātana dharma*, the eternal religion. It is not to be identified with any particular religion, for it is the religion which transcends race and creed and yet informs all races and creeds. We can so transform the religion to which we belong as to make it approximate to the religion of spirit.[25]

Radhakrishnan presents his *sanātana dharma* as a faith with few dogmas. Consider his 1942 Kamala Lecture at the University of Calcutta :

24. IVL, 125-126.
25. RF, 204.

> The essence of religion is not in the dogmas and creeds, in the rites and ceremonies which repel many of us, but in the deepest wisdom of the ages, the *philosophia perennis*, sanātana dharma, which is the only guide through the bewildering chaos of modern thought.[26]

Radhakrishnan's faith attracts those who seek "the deepest wisdom of the ages," who shy away from dogmas and creeds, rites and ceremonies. They agree with him that "there is a common ground on which the different religious traditions rest."[27] Radhakrishnan repeatedly refers to this common ground as "the religion of spirit," a designation aimed at transcending symbolic and propositional specificity.

One thread running throughout the tapestry of Radhakrishnan's faith (1) is his attitude of conviction that the world rests on spirit. He describes the Hindu spirit as "that attitude towards life which regards the endless variety of the visible and the temporal world as sustained and supported by the invisible and eternal spirit."[28] No element of his religious thought is more central to Radhakrishnan's *māyā* hermeneutics. He calls the essence of religion "the vision of a reality which stands beyond and within the passing flux of immediate things, the intuitive loyalty to something larger than and beyond oneself."[29] He thinks reality is a spiritual whole which includes what is beyond and within the world, the invisible and the visible, the eternal and the temporal. The parts (world) are real, but only as parts of a comprehensive and inclusive whole. In short, they are real only as they rest on spirit.

Another thread is seen in Radhakrishnan's description of that for which India stands : "she stands for an eternal principle—that life is a spiritual aspiration, matter the handiwork of spirit, and all the universe one in spirit."[30] He regards oneness in spirit to be both actual and potential, both an ontological fact and a teleological ideal. Radhakrishnan reports that "this ultimate oneness of things is what the Hindu is required to remember

26. RS, 43.
27. OSW, 1952-1959, 292.
28. HVL, 88.
29. D, 35.
30. PRT, 292.

every moment of his life."[31] Remembering an alleged ultimate oneness of things, in Radhakrishnan's view, can organize and integrate a human self, set its direction, and guide all its actions.[32]

Radhakrishnan's faith (2) is his symbol-system for expressing and communicating his faith (1). Brahman, Īśvara, and Hiraṇya-garbha are among the most important symbols in Radhakrishnan's faith (2) and they have already been encountered in chapter two. In a pivotal discussion of *māyā* Radhakrishnan advises :

> If we keep in mind the fourfold character of the Supreme, we shall avoid confusion in regard to the status of the world. If we concentrate attention on *Brahman*, the Absolute, we feel that the world is not independent of *Brahman* but rests in *Brahman*. The relationship between the two cannot be logically articulated. If we turn to the personal *Īśvara*, we know that the world is the creation of *Brahman* and not its organic expression. The power of creation is called *māyā*. If we turn to the world process which is a perpetual becoming, it is a mixture of being and non-being, *sat* and *asat*, the divine principle and *prakṛti*. *Hiraṇya-garbha* and his world are both subject to time, and should be distinguished from the eternal. But the temporal becoming is by no means false.[33]

Brahman, poise one, expresses and communicates his attitude of conviction about the ultimate oneness of things. *Brahman* cannot state the nature of the case in a propositional way since statements regarding the nature of Brahman are precluded by the Upaniṣadic idea *neti neti*. *Brahman*, like all symbols, can only suggest a reality beyond itself in which it also participates. Yet the power of religious symbols should never be underestimated. The symbol *Īśvara*, poise two, expresses Radhakrishnan's attitude of conviction regarding personal agency, a personal God. *Īśvara's* power of self-becoming is signified by what this study calls *māyā*². The cosmogonic Puruṣa Sūkta, *Ṛg Veda* X.90, portrays Puruṣa (*Īśvara*) becoming (not "creating") the world (*Virāṭ*)

31. PRT, 25.
32. The "self" is a key term in Hutchison's definition of faith, yet the concept of "self" differs in Eastern and Western ways of thinking. This important cross-cultural issue can only be recognized here, not examined.
33. PU, 90.

through the power of self-becoming. *Hiranyagarbha*, poise three, is a symbol which communicates Radhakrishnan's conviction regarding a world-soul.

The reader's attention is invited to just one more symbol, *Brahman-Ātman*. It expresses Radhakrishnan's attitude of conviction that "the larger environment is of the nature of one's own self." Many words would be required to state the wide-ranging implications of this key element in Radhakrishnan's faith (1). For instance, it implies *tat tvam asi* (*Chāndogya Upaniṣad* VI.8-16). It implies that the four states of consciousness (*Māṇḍūkya Upaniṣad*) correspond with Radhakrishnan's four poises of reality. It implies the mysticism of ontological union between the self and all beings (*Īśa Upaniṣad* 7). Yet just two words used symbolically—*Brahman-Ātman*—can express and communicate what would otherwise require many statements.

Faith (3) in Radhakrishnan consists of his beliefs, his faith (1) and his faith (2) become propositional. President Radhakrishnan delivered an address at the Indian Institute of Advanced Study, Simla, on 20 October 1965 in which he characterized the four different *Vedas* as having four *Mahāvākyas* ("Great Sayings"): "*prajñānaṁ brahma* (The intelligence is Divine), *ayamātmā brahma* (The soul is Divine), *aham brahmāsmi* (I am Divine), *tattvamasi* (That art Thou)."[34] These four Mahāvākyas are foundation stones of Radhakrishnan's faith (3). Whether *aham brahmāsmi* is translated "I am Brahman" or "I am Divine," it is still a statement of belief, a religious proposition. Identifying two kinds of religious persons, mystics and non-mystics, Radhakrishnan goes on to show quite correctly that "There is a world of difference between those who say *asti brahma* and those who say *aham brahmāsmi*."[35] This statement indicates that belief or faith (3) *does* make a difference to Radhakrishnan despite his many disclaimer affidavits regarding dogmas and creeds. It could be shown that *aham brahmāsmi* is an essential part of his "Church"[36] dogmatics.

34. PRSW, Second Series, 124.

35. Ibid., 114.

36. Cf. "True religion is not what we get from outside, from books and teachers. It is the aspiration of the human soul, that which unfolds within oneself, that which is built by one's life blood. Those who follow this view are

The Vedic saying *tat tvam asi* (That art thou) is a well-known Hindu belief and an essential ingredient of Radhakrishnan's faith (3). He claims : "The great text, *Tat tvam asi*, That art thou, is the simple statement of an experienced fact,"[37] citing the Sanskrit phrase often.[38] This "experienced fact" is as certain for Radhakrishnan as the reader's experience of the fact that there are black letters on this white page. There are many variations on the theme *tat tvam asi* such as "man is but the localised expression of God"[39] and "When the highest perfection is reached, the rhythm of man's life becomes one with that of the cosmic spirit."[40] Radhakrishnan is convinced that "it is impossible for man, a child of eternity, to distinguish himself from God in the long run,"[41] and that "the inner immortal self and the great cosmic power are one and the same."[42] Radhakrishnan believes that we are "God-men,"[43] what might be referred to better as "God-persons." He says the Hindu "believes that God may be incarnated in any man, even as He was in Jesus or Buddha."[44] Discussing the life of the reborn, Radhakrishnan remarks :

> These rare and precious souls, filled with the spirit of the whole, may be said to be world-conscious. They have the vision of the self in all existences and of all existences in the self. 'The three worlds are my native home,' declares the Hindu sage.[45]

Radhakrishnan connects the belief in *tat tvam asi* with "world-consciousness," believing the sage should relate to reality in each

the seers. They belong to a single family though they dwell in spaces far apart. They belong to the open, unorganized community, the invisible Church of Spirit, whose membership is scattered over the whole earth." (RF, 143).

37. HH, 63.
38. See IP, I, 170; HH, 86, 100; IVL, 104; OSW, 1952-1959, 288.
39. PRT, 111.
40. PRT, 114.
41. RRCP, 424.
42. IP, I, 146.
43. IVL, 158. Thomas Paul Urumpackal discusses "God-men" in *Organized Religion According to Dr. S. Radhakrishnan* (Rome: Universita Gregoriana Editrice, 1972), pp. 40-44.
44. HH, 7.
45. IVL, 116.

of its four poises. Therefore, the sage should be at home in the secular world. Radhakrishnan believes with great conviction that "the self is not sharply marked off from the world."[46] *Īśa Upaniṣad* 6 and 7 support his view. Many more illustrations could be cited, but the point is very simple. Any interpretation of *māyā* must take into account the wide-ranging implications of *tat tvam asi*.

Some of Radhakrishnan's strongest beliefs are in the area of ethics. In his view, the relation between an individual and society is shaped by the threefold discipline signified by *puruṣa-artha*, *varṇa*, and *āśrama* :

> The Hindu view of the individual and his relation to society can be best brought out by a reference to the synthesis and gradation of (i) the fourfold object of life (*puruṣārtha*), desire and enjoyment (*kāma*), interest (*artha*) ethical living (*dharma*), and spiritual freedom (*mokṣa*); (ii) the fourfold order of society (*varṇa*), the man of learning (*Brāhmin*), of power (*Kṣatriya*), of skilled productivity (*Vaiśya*), and of service (*Śūdra*); and (iii) the fourfold succession of the stages of life (*āśrama*), student (*brahmacāri*), householder (*grihastha*), forest recluse (*vānaprastha*), and the free supersocial man (*sannyāsin*).[47]

Kāma, the first *puruṣārtha* listed, means erotic pleasure and aesthetic enjoyment. Vātsyāyana's *Kāmasūtra* is the classical text. *Artha* means "material advantage which includes political and economic power."[48] Kauṭilya's *Arthaśāstra* is the classical text. Radhakrishnan makes an astounding understatement about the next *puruṣārtha* : "Dharma is a word of protean significance."[49] *Varṇa*, whose etymology suggests "color," is the word for caste. *The Code of Manu* describes the general pattern of social order. Radhakrishnan's *māyā* hermeneutics is directly related to his interpretation of Hindu social ethics. However, a complete study of

46. IVL, 211.

47. ERWT, 331. Cf. ERWT, 67; RS, 72.

48. S. Radhakrishnan and Charles A. Moore, eds., *A Source book in Indian Philosophy*, p. 193.

49. RS, 107. On the meanings of the word *dharma*, cf. PRT, 83-84; HH, 17, 32; HVL, 56. An excellent exposition of the meanings of *dharma* is found in Austin B. Creel, *Dharma in Hindu Ethics* (Columbia, Missouri: South Asia Books, 1977).

Radhakrishnan's ethics would be required in order to apply his *māyā* hermeneutics to each of the twelve items contained in the above passage.[50] The main point here is that Radhakrishnan's faith (3) includes very specific beliefs regarding ethics and society.

Radhakrishnan's writings contain other passages[51] which list his faith (3) such as:

> For the first time in the history of thought, the Upaniṣads indicate a religious view which has for its integral elements: the supremacy of the Absolute spirit; the reality of mystic consciousness; the distinction between intellect soberly contemplating the intelligible and intellect rapt into enthusiasm and borne above itself; higher and lower knowledge; the *via negativa* as the way of approach to the mystic consciousness; the non-ultimateness of the pluralistic universe with its independent existents, some with life, some with consciousness; insistence on ascetic discipline; rebirth determined by the law of Karma, until the destiny of man is realized which is release or deliverance.[52]

Since Radhakrishnan accepts the authority of the Upaniṣads, it is safe to assume that these eight Upaniṣadic elements are also elements in Radhakrishnan's faith. All three aspects of his faith shine through but only the propositional beliefs are of interest here. Radhakrishnan believes there is an "Absolute spirit," separating himself from materialists. He posits "the reality of mystic consciousness,"[53] a religious theme paralleling his philosophical presupposition that consciousness has ontological status. Radhakrishnan believes in "rebirth determined by the law of Karma." It is noteworthy that *Karma* and *Absolute* are the only unusually capitalized words, indicating that they signify particularly important beliefs.[54] It also indicates that they are religious symbols. Finally, Radhakrishnan believes that a person's destiny is "re-

50. Aloysius Michael, *Radhakrishnan on Hindu Moral Life and Action* (Delhi: Concept Publishing Company, 1979).

51. Kalki, 54; ERWT, 296; IC, 120; RF, 204; OH, 85.

52. ERWT, 133.

53. On mysticism see "Religion and Life," 96; PRT, 80; RRCP, 22, 38, 263; IP, I, 262; RWN, 24-25; ERWT, 109; RS, 49; BS, 109-110.

54. On *karma* and *saṃsāra* see PRT, 86, 223, 246-247; RRCP, 449; HH, 7-8, 110; IP, I, 249; IP, II, 150; IVL, 275, 290; PU, 114.

lease or deliverance" (*mokṣa*), a position separating him from fatalists, nihilists, and other pessimists.

Summarizing this introduction to three aspects of S. Radhakrishnan's faith, there are many threads in the tapestry of his faith (1). He has the attitude of conviction that there is a mode of consciousness which carries with it self-evidence and completeness. He affirms his faith in the identity of one's own true self with the larger environment. He calls his own religion *sanātana dharma*, the eternal religion, the religion of spirit. These phrases are relatively free of the symbolic and propositional specificity which Radhakrishnan tries to avoid. He affirms that the world rests on spirit. He is convinced that the ultimate oneness of things is both an ontological fact and a teleological ideal. Radhakrishnan's faith (2) consists of a complex network of inter-connected symbols including four primary symbols: Brahman, *Īśvara*, *Hiraṇyagarbha*, and *Virāṭ*. Other symbols can be connected to each of these in many ways. For instance, māyā² described in the next chapter is *Īśvara's* power of self-becoming. *Brahman-Ātman* expresses and communicates Radhakrishnan's attitude of conviction that there is an identity between one's own true self and the larger environment. The two words *Brahman-Ātman* are a particularly good illustration of the power of symbols. Finally, Radhakrishnan's faith (3) is his belief system. It includes the propositions *aham brahmāsmi* (I am Brahman) and *tat tvam asi* (that art thou). It also includes belief in the efficacy of the threefold discipline signified by *puruṣārtha*, *varṇa*, and *āśrama*. Finally, it includes belief in: an Absolute spirit; the reality of mystic consciousness; rebirth determined by the law of Karma; and release or deliverance (*mokṣa*).

III. The Unity of Religions

This section describes Radhakrishnan's position regarding an alleged unity of religions. It takes up: (1) his admonition that we stick to religion and let religions go; (2) his view that Hinduism has no fixed creed; (3) his diagnosis that we suffer from the disease of dogmatism; and (4) his hope that tolerance will establish concord (*samavāya*) not only among religions but in every sphere of life.

First, Radhakrishnan wholeheartedly agrees with Rabindranath Tagore whose religious message is supposedly simple: "Stick to religion, let religions go."[55] In 1918, five years after Tagore received the Nobel Peace Prize for Literature, Radhakrishnan wrote: "The popularity of the writings of Sir Rabindranath Tagore shows that there is neither East nor West in the realm of spirit."[56] Those who agree with Tagore and Radhakrishnan throw the religions of the world into a melting pot. Those who disagree might toss them into a salad bowl. Radhakrishnan's supporters choose to melt down the specificity of particular religious symbols and beliefs. His detractors choose to maintain religious diversity with its historical particularity. They enjoy tossed salad in which tomatoes and lettuce retain their own identities.

Many passages illustrate Radhakrishnan's faith regarding the alleged unity of religions. He thinks "there is a common substratum from which all religions spring."[57] He states: "All religions are intertwined at the roots and meet at the summit."[58] In good melting-pot fashion he writes: "the harmony of all descriptions is the essential fact of our religion."[59] His detractors take issue with each of these claims. In direct opposition to *advaita vedānta*, they choose to remember and be guided by the ultimate "non-oneness" of things including the non-oneness of religious faiths.

Radhakrishnan's faith in the unity of religions rests on his philosophy of "this and that." He writes:

> The philosophy of this and that indicates that God has not left Himself without a witness among any people....
>
> Today, we have come to realize the unwisdom of the policy of this or that.[60]

Radhakrishnan's philosophy of this and that is influenced by the Jaina epistemological theory of *saptabhaṅgī* (predication in "seven forms"). The philosophy of this and that encourages inclusive ways of thinking; it discourages exclusive ways of thinking. It is incompatible with the Greek philosophy of this or that.

55. PRT, 177.
56. PRT, "Preface," vii.
57. PRSW, Second Series, 129.
58. OSW, 1952-1959, 90.
59. PRSW, Second Series, 136.
60. PCF. 154.

Radhakrishnan says "the Hindu tradition believes that the different views are complementary."[61] He applies this principle of complementarity not only to the orthodox and heterodox faiths of India but also to cumulative traditions and faiths from around the world. Over and over, again and again, Radhakrishnan makes the point which is illustrated by the famous elephant fable[62] in which four blind persons (according to one version) or four persons in a dark shed (according to another) describe an elephant in four different ways because each person touches a different part of the elephant. Although there seem to be different religions when we study religious phenomena from our separate points of view, says Radhakrishnan, there is actually only one religion just as there is actually only one elephant.

Radhakrishnan says his position regarding the unity of religions is not that they should merge into one religion, admitting that "A single religion for all mankind will take away from the spiritual richness of the world."[63] Claiming he is not a syncretist, Radhakrishnan says he wants to honor religious particularities:

> We do not wish to eliminate the particular elements in different religions. Beliefs are the codified expressions of experience. Religious traditions, rites and ceremonies do not grow in a void. They have roots in the soil and they are nourished by the same life-giving and life-sustaining elements. We accept differences and try to understand them. We do not encourage the effort to recast the world in any one image. We do not believe in any religious Esperanto.
>
> Though our thinking is international or global our particular commitments, so long as they are not injurious to human fellowship, should be fostered.[64]

Two important points should be noted. First, Radhakrishnan says he wants to foster particular religious commitments "so long as they are not injurious to human fellowship." We would do well to apply this standard whenever our own religious commit-

61. BG, 20.
62. See EW, 32-33.
63. Kalki, 46-47. Cf. "The world is seeking not so much a fusion of religions as a fellowship of religions." (Schilpp, ed., 75).
64. FS, 9.

ment begins to get in the way of our fellowship with other persons. Second, Radhakrishnan's affirmation of differences among religions is set alongside his proposition that different religions "have their roots in the soil" and are "nourished by the same life-giving and life-sustaining elements." Radhakrishnan's argument rests on the assumption that "soil" is the same everywhere, that all soil contains the same elements. It is fair for Radhakrishnan's detractors to ask for the reason why soil on all seven continents should be expected to contain the same percentages of phosphate, nitrogen, and other elements. Radhakrishnan's unity of religions is as paradoxical as his "one" which is not singular. His admonition that we stick to religion and let religions go recalls Akbar's creed, Dīn-i-Ilāhi, which was hammered out in the Hall of Worship at Fatehpur Sikri. Radhakrishnan writes: "Akbar's attempt failed because it was not a living synthesis but an intellectual eclecticism."[65] The fate of Radhakrishnan's synthesis depends on whether it becomes a synthesis throbbing with passion and life or just another arid exercise in intellectual eclecticism.

Second, Radhakrishnan claims that Hinduism is not bound up with a creed. The unity of religions which he envisions would certainly be attractive if it were true that Hinduism is ultimately creedless. Radhakrishnan argues that:

> Hinduism has no fixed creed by which it may be said to stand or fall, for it is convinced that the spirit will outgrow the creed. For the Hindu every religion is true, if only its adherents sincerely and honestly follow it....Hinduism is not bound up with a creed or a book, a prophet or a founder, but is persistent search for truth on the basis of a continuously renewed experience. Hinduism is human thought about God in continuous evolution.[66]

Radhakrishnan is careful to say that Hinduism has no *fixed* creed. It is not *bound up* with a creed. Elsewhere he explains that "Hindus believe in the relativity of creeds to the general character of the people who profess them."[67] The relativity of creeds implies that

65. FS, 19.

66. RS, 53-54. Cf. "Hinduism is a movement, not a position; a process, not a result; a growing tradition, not a fixed revelation." (HVL, 91) An earlier version of this statement appears in HH, 27.

67. HH, 4. Cf. "It is impossible to pledge ourselves to an inflexible creed."

there *are* creeds. Radhakrishnan's view is that creeds come and go but the spirit underlying them lasts forever. He is thoroughly convinced that in the final analysis his religion of spirit will end competition among the world's religions. He has complete faith in the underlying unity of religions despite the diversity of their creeds.

Third, Radhakrishnan's faith contains the recurring theme that humankind has been afflicted by dogmatism. He thinks "the world has bled and suffered from the disease of dogmatism, of conformity, of intolerance."[68] Remaining loyal to his own tradition, he attests that "Naturally the Upaniṣads do not adopt an attitude of dogmatism."[69] He is convinced that the disease of dogmatism can be cured. On 23 May 1956, Radhakrishnan made a speech at the laying of the foundation stone for the Buddha Memorial in Delhi. He spoke of the Buddha, one of humanity's great healers:

> In the spirit of this country, he pointed out that the highest spiritual freedom is incapable of doctrinal formulation....The Buddha has no opinions, for he has seen. His declarations come fresh and breathless, hot and glistening from the baptism of inner experience. He has a great shyness, a profound reticence. An experience is not a theory. He rejects the contending formulas of the intellect as inadequate either to lead to or express the paradoxical truth. The inward spirit of truth challenges all forms. Language makes reality more articulate than it is. Language is at best an instrument and like all instruments subject to imperfection. The doctrines are rebuked, defeated and swallowed up again in experience. We must see before we say.[70]

Radhakrishnan separates religious experience from expressions and statements of religious experience, faith (1) from faith (2) and faith (3). His cure for the disease of dogmatism is to subordinate particular symbols and specific beliefs to the attitudes of conviction which they express and state, respectively. Radhakrishnan

(IP, I, 304) Elsewhere he warns us not to "bind our eyes from further seeking with the bandage of a final creed." (Schilpp, ed., 54)

68. OSW, 1952-1959, 335.
69. PU, 143-144.
70. OSW, 1952-1959, 348.

admires the Buddha because he rebuked doctrines and swallowed them up again in experiential fact. The Buddha's experience at Bodhgaya is the one fact about which all Buddhists agree. The Buddha is reported to have said that metaphysical questions are unedifying. In the same spirit, Radhakrishnan admonishes his readers to remember the alleged ultimate oneness of things. He thinks this attitude of conviction will cure the disease of dogmatism and thereby foster the unity of religions.

Finally, Radhakrishnan hopes that tolerance will establish concord (*samavāya*) not only among religions but in every sphere of life. In his autobiographical essay "My Search For Truth" he narrates:

> My religious sense did not allow me to speak a rash or a profane word of anything which the soul of man holds or has held sacred. This attitude of respect for all creeds, this elementary good manners in matters of spirit, is bred into the marrow of one's bones by the Hindu tradition, by its experience of centuries. Religious tolerance marked the Hindu culture from its very beginnings.[71]

Radhakrishnan's view is that the unity of religions is a creative operative force (an ideal) which shapes the process of events entire. It elicits spiritual good manners. Discussing UNESCO's underlying belief in tolerance, Radhakrishnan gives us a definition which is useful in all spheres of life:

> Tolerance is not indifference, but that most precious and difficult quality of impartiality that combines loyalty to one's own convictions with respect and fairness for the convictions of those who passionately adhere to other views.[73]

Elsewhere Radhakrishnan says we must "learn to be loyal to the spirit of loyalty in other people."[73] He hopes that loyalty to our own religious traditions will be combined with deep respect for the faith and cumulative traditions of others. Hajime Naka-

71. Ferm, ed., *Religion in Transition*, 17. Cf. "The Hindu leaders from the times of the Upaniṣads have asked us to be tolerant even with the intolerant." (EWR, 110)

72. S. Radhakrishnan, "UNESCO and World Revolution," *The New Republic* 123 (10 July 1950): 15.

73. ERWT, 338.

mura observes that "Generally speaking, we *cannot find in any Indian religion the conception of heretic*' in the sense of Western usage."[74]

Whether Nakamura is right or wrong, there can be no doubt about the fact that Radhakrishnan hopes tolerance will establish concord. References to concord (*samavāya*) appear especially in his later writings:

> Inter-cultural, inter-religious co-operation has been taking place in India from the beginning of her history, with its central principle formulated by Aśoka in his XIIth rock edict—*samavāya eva sādhuḥ*. Concord alone is meritorious.[75]

Radhakrishnan often cites[76] King Aśoka's Rock Edict XII which can be visited today in the Dhaulī Hills near Bhubaneshwar, Orissa:

> Interreligious understanding is native to India. Aśoka in his twelfth edict proclaimed:
>
> He who does reverence to his own sect, while disparaging the sects of others, wholly from attachment to his own, with intent to enhance the glory of his own sect, in reality, by such conduct, inflicts the severest injury on his own sect. Concord, therefore, is meritorious, to wit, hearkening and hearkening willingly to the law of piety as accepted by other people.[77]

Radhakrishnan holds the laudable view that concord is meritorious not only among sects and religions but also among nations, races, and political blocs. His work in the League of Nations and the United Nations testifies to this. While the Buddha claims that ignorant craving causes human suffering, Radhakrishnan argues that "conflict is at the root of man's misery."[78] He was utterly convinced that "man cannot rest in an unresolved discord."[79] In his view, conflict and discord disappear when the conflicting, discordant parts are seen as parts of the whole, when people "see" an alleged ultimate oneness of things.

74. Hajime Nakamura, *Ways of Thinking of Eastern Peoples* (Honolulu: East-West Center Press, 1964), p. 170.
75. PRSW, Second Series, 362.
76. See OSW, 1952-1959, 337, 363; PRSW, Second Series, 136; OH, 10.
77. RC, 19.
78. D, 16.
79. WUS, 3.

In short, Radhakrishnan along with Tagore would have people stick to religion and let religions go. A philosophy of "this and that" rather than "this or that" underlies their faith in the unity of religions. He suggests that Hinduism is not bound up with a creed and that most people are suffering from the disease of dogmatism. Finally, he would like to see tolerance at all levels lead to the establishment of deep, lasting concord.

IV. A Modernist's Loyalty to Tradition

This section describes Radhakrishnan's attitude toward tradition. In the "Preface" to his translation of *The Brahma Sūtra* Radhakrishnan explains: "It is my endeavour to present a reasoned faith which deals with the old Indian tradition and the demands of modern thought."[80] Clearly he is a modernist. His loyalty to tradition is balanced by his loyalty to novel ideas. A modernist is someone who fits Radhakrishnan's description of Śaṅkara in his age: "The age needed a religious genius who was unwilling to break with the past and yet open to the good influences of the new creeds, one who could stretch the old moulds without breaking them."[81] Radhakrishnan's attitude toward tradition is that we should stretch the old molds. Stretching them precludes either using them as they are or discarding them. As a modernist, Radhakrishnan stretches the Hindu mold of *māyā*.

Radhakrishnan displays great respect for tradition as evidenced in his well-known statement that "It takes centuries of life to make a little history, and it takes centuries of history to produce a little tradition, and we cannot lightly set it aside."[82] He also has a modernist's respect for freedom, declaring that "Loyalty to our particular tradition means not only concord with the past but also freedom from the past."[83] Some of his best traditional-modernist statements are contained in *Freedom and Culture*, an almost unattainable collection of addresses delivered before uni-

80. BS, 11.

81. IP, II, 467. Elsewhere Radhakrishnan writes: "I hope that love of ease, regard for antiquity or considerations of safety will not induce us to spare the ancient moulds, however beautiful, when they are outworn." (FC, 10)

82. IVL, 78-79.

83. PU, 145.

versity audiences. He cautions that "Your education has been in vain if you are not protected from the dangers of dogmatics. No opinion is true simply because it is handed down from the past, and we cling to it with passion."[84] Prabhu Dutt Shastri's illusional interpretation of *māyā* would be no exception. Elsewhere Radhakrishnan compares loyalty to tradition with memory: "Just as each individual strives to organise his memory, we have to organise our past."[85] Radhakrishnan's modernism is that of a traditionalist and his *māyā* hermeneutics shows respect for a traditional form.

Radhakrishnan's respect for tradition does not require him to defend dead forms and obsolete watchwords. To the contrary, the power of his pen for producing florid prose is brought to bear on those who think that something is venerable simply because it is ancient:

> To-day a great mass of accretions have accumulated, which are choking up the stream and the free life of spirit. To say that the dead forms, which have no vital truth to support them, are too ancient and venerable to be tampered with, only prolongs the suffering of the patient who is ailing from the poison generated by the putrid waste of the past. The conservative mind must open itself to the necessity of change.[86]

What should we do about these accretions ? Elsewhere Radhakrishnan exhorts, "We must free ourselves from all the exhausted traditions, spent forces, and obsolete watchwords which still possess us."[87] He does not think we should free ourselves from all traditions, only from all *exhausted* traditions. A purpose of this study is to determine the extent to which Radhakrishnan thinks *māyā* is an obsolete watchword, an exhausted tradition.

84. FC, 75.

85. BS, 12. Cf. "A man is not himself without his memory. What is true of individuals is true of peoples." (FC, 95)

86. IP, II, 777. Cf. "Stagnant systems, like pools, breed obnoxious growths, while flowing rivers constantly renew their waters from fresh springs of inspiration." (IP, II, 780) See also FC, 10-11. Cf. "God does not say 'I am Tradition', but he says 'I am Truth'." ("My Search for Truth," in *Radhakrishnan*, ed., McDermott, p. 45.)

87. PRT, 180. Cf. "If we are wedded overmuch to the rules of the past, if the living faith of the dead becomes the dead faith of the living, the civilisation will die." (RS, 117) Cf. also EWR, 104-105.

As a modernist, Radhakrishnan is imbued with the idea of liberty. In his view, liberty and freedom are what the Hindu tradition is all about. It would be the epitome of irony to see this tradition of freedom and liberty strangle itself by uncritical loyalty to itself. In the last pages of his book on Tagore (1918), Radhakrishnan wrote a passage with which it seems fitting and proper to end this section on a modernist's loyalty to tradition:

> All the world over the spirit of freedom is awake. But where is India ? Can she alone remain immune from its contagion ? Can she alone remain unshaken by a passion which is so universal in its power over men ? Rise, India ! Break up the spell of old tradition, cut off the meshes of despotism and return to the ancient though despised ideals of spirit and liberty.[88]

V. Ethics

The relationship between *māyā* hermeneutics and ethics becomes crystal clear in Radhakrishnan's question: "Is the moral ideal a dream and am I fighting only a sham fight against the tremendous forces of evil and wickedness ?"[89] Beginning in 1908 when he submitted his M.A. thesis entitled *Ethics of the Vedānta*, Radhakrishnan argued tirelessly that the Vedānta system includes room for a positive ethic.[90] He reminisces that "My occasional contributions to learned magazines like the *International Journal of Ethics*, *Monist*, *Quest*, had for their objective the establishing of the ethical character of the Hindu religion."[91] For instance, Radhakrishnan's 1937 Sir George Birdwood Memorial Lecture[92] before the Royal Society of Arts in London entitled "Mysticism and Ethics in Hindu Thought" is a point for point refutation[93] of the dichot-

88. PRT, 293-294.
89. "Religion and Life," 93.
90. Ferm, ed., *Religion in Transition*, p. 19.
91. Ibid., p. 22.
92. Available in ERWT, 58-114.
93. He lists eight points, ERWT, 76. According to Radhakrishnan, Schweitzer's third point is : "(3) The Hindu doctrine of *māyā*, which declares that life is an illusion, contains the flaw of world and life negation, and in consequence Hindu thought is non-ethical."

omy alleged by Albert Schweitzer[94] between Christian "world and life affirmation" and Hindu "world and life negation."

This section considers five recurring ethical themes in Radhakrishnan's thought: (1) the relation between ethics and metaphysics; (2) situation ethics; (3) non-attachment to objects of the world; (4) saving the world; and (5) the organic relationship between the religious spirit and an active life.

First of all, Radhakrishnan calls for ethics to be deeply rooted in metaphysics:

> We cannot help asking ourselves whether our ideals are mere private dreams of our own or bonds created by society, or even aspirations characteristic of the human species. Only a philosophy which affirms that they are rooted in the universal nature of things can give depth and fervour to moral life, courage and confidence in moral difficulties. We need to be fortified by the conviction that the service of the ideals is what the cosmic scheme demands of us, that our loyalty or disloyalty to them is a matter of the deepest moment not only to ourselves or to society , or even to the human species, but to the nature of things.[95]

What is the nature of things ? Radhakrishnan thinks the universal nature of things cannot be grasped in its entirety by the discursive intellect. Yet in so far as he ventures to describe the indescribable, he names it unity, continuity, consciousness, the whole, harmony and truth. These ontological concepts and Radhakrishnan's ethical ideals would have to correspond point for point in order for us to say that his intellectual architectonic is coherent. Making such a judgment would require an entire project on the relation between his ethics and his metaphysics.[96] The point here is that Radhakrishnan thinks the ethically ideal *should be* rooted in the ontologically real.

94. In his book *Indian Thought and Its Development* (London: Hodder and Stoughton Ltd., 1936; reprinted, London: Adam and Charles Black, 1951).

95. ERWT, 82. Cf. "Any ethical theory must be grounded in metaphysics, in a philosophical conception of the relation between human conduct and ultimate reality. As we think ultimate reality to be, so we behave. Vision and action go together. If we believe absurdities, we shall commit atrocities." (ERWT, 80) Cf. also "Belief and behaviour go together." (RF, 8).

96. Cf. Charles A. Moore, "Metaphysics and Ethics in Radhakrishnan's Philosophy," in *The Philosophy of Sarvepalli Radhakrishnan*, ed. Paul Arthur Schilpp (New York: Tudor Publishing Company, 1952), pp. 281-312.

In situation ethics, judgments are made by giving equal weight to the demands of a particular situation and the ethical rule or principle which is to be applied in that particular situation. While Radhakrishnan never uses the phrase "situation ethics," his 1942 Kamala Lectures at the Universities of Calcutta and Benares contain evidence that he is a situational ethicist. Published as *Religion and Society*, they are the best primary source for Radhakrishnan's ideas on the subject he chose: "social reconstruction in the light of religious ideals."[97] His restlessness regarding unexamined social practices transmitted down through the centuries is evident as he addresses the ethical problem of determining the demands of *dharma*:

> Though dharma is absolute, it has no absolute and timeless content. The only thing eternal about morality is man's desire for the better. But time and circumstances determine what the 'better' is in each situation. We cannot elevate social conventions into absolute rules, without taking into account the concrete attendent circumstances. There is no positive human action that can be pronounced *a priori* to be absolutely right or wrong, wholly without regard to the circumstances in which it is done.[98]

It follows that Radhakrishnan considers the threefold discipline signified by *puruṣārtha*, *varṇa*, and *āśrama* to be absolute although it need not necessarily have any absolute and timeless content. During his Kamala Lectures, the world was at war and India's armies were fighting bravely against the Axis Powers. With Japanese armies moving westward across Southeast Asia, Radhakrishnan was saying in Calcutta:

> The Hindu scriptures look upon ahiṁsā, or non-violence, as the highest virtue....But we cannot say that the Hindu scriptures require us to avoid the use of force altogether. The Hindu view does not sternly uphold a distant ideal, while condemning all compromises with it. The divine is not to be found in detachment from the common life. The concrete

97. RS, 9.
98. RS, 114.

> demands of each particular situation are studied, and the principle adapted to it.[99]

It would be interesting to know how Gandhi might have reacted to this statement regarding *ahiṃsā*. Probably he would have given more weight to the *ahiṃsā* principle than to the situation in which the ethical principle was to be applied.

In the third place, Radhakrishnan recommends action in a spirit of non-attachment to objects of the world. He thinks the Upaniṣads "insist on a spirit of detachment, *vairāgya*, which is not indifference to the world. It is not abandonment of objects but non-attachment to them."[100] A recurring theme in S. Radhakrishnan's faith is that action in the world should be taken without forgetting the ultimate oneness of things. If things are ultimately one, it is also the case that (1) there is no real separation between us and Brahman and (2) there is no real separation between us and the world. Radhakrishnan is deeply convinced that our relationship to the world should parallel our relationship to Brahman. He recommends achieving union with both poises of reality since the world is no more illusory than Brahman even though Brahman is more inclusive. Describing the teachings of the *Bhagavadgītā*, Radhakrishnan declares that "Right through, the teacher emphasizes the need for action. He does not adopt the solution of dismissing the world as an illusion and action as a snare."[101] Action is not a snare if we remain non-attached to the fruits of action. Radhakrishnan explains: "Hindu thought points out that what binds is not action but the spirit in which it is done. It is the desire for or aversion from the results that binds the individual soul."[102] Radhakrishnan thinks desire for or aversion from *anything* violates the spirit of non-attachment to objects of the world, attesting that "True asceticism is not indifference to the suffering of the world, but the building up of a silent centre even in the furious activity of life."[103] In his view, furious activity is compatible with a spirit of non-attachment.

99. RS, 201. Cf. "We have to mediate between the supreme ideal of absolute non-violence and the actual conditions." (RS, 204)

100. PU, 106.

101. BG, 66.

102. BS, 217.

103. IP, I, 587-588.

Fourthly, Radhakrishnan formulated his *māyā* hermeneutics in order "to save the world and give to it a real meaning."[104] The phrase "to save the world" in this context means to articulate an ontological vision of the world in which the world has value and meaning. In an ethical context, "to save the world" means something related but different. Radhakrishnan proclaims that "One who has completely shaken himself free from selfishness is at liberty to take upon himself the task of the world. His attitude will be not world-seeking or world-fleeing, but world-saving."[105] Ethical seriousness steers a middle course between desire for and withdrawal from the tasks of the world. Elsewhere Radhakrishnan observes that "The essence of moral life consists not so much in adjusting ourselves to the environment as in transforming it so that it may embody our ideals to a larger and larger extent."[106] It would be interesting to use this statement as the basis for analyzing the moral struggles of the village peasant Hori, a character in Premchand's Hindi novel *Godaan* (*The Gift of a Cow*). A recurring theme in S. Radhakrishnan's faith is that saving the world means transforming one's environment. Transforming it would be difficult without living in it. Radhakrishnan is convinced that "no one who holds himself aloof from the activities of the world and who is insensitive to its woes can be really wise."[107] On the other hand, he does not think the answer is to be immersed completely in the furious activities of the world, writing that "a truly religious man lives on the frontiers between the sacred and the secular."[108] "Sanctity or holiness is not unworldliness, it is participation in the agony of the world with a proper frame of mind,"[109] and such participation requires a deep conviction that the world is *not* an illusion.

104. See Appendix V.

105. IP, II, 633.

106. Kalki, 52. Cf. "Religion is not only life-transcending but also life-transforming." (EWR, 69) Cf. also "The liberated soul of the true saint does not wish to escape from this world but tries to improve it." (PRT, 80)

107. EWR, 137. Cf. "We can realise the divinity within us not by the contemplation of the 'starry heavens above' or 'the moral law within' but only by entering into the stream of things." ("Religion and Life," 102)

108. RCW, 110. Cf. RF, 23. Paul Tillich's book title *On the Boundary* comes to mind.

109. PRSW, Second Series, 129.

Finally, Radhakrishnan sees an organic relationship between the religious spirit and an active life. He states this view passionately and impatiently in his 1916 article "Religion and Life," commenting on the three million ascetics who were then wandering all over India:

> Many of these are poor beggars who deceive the public by putting on the ascetic's garb....But a large proportion of these three millions will be men of a fairly high degree of intelligence, a good deal of selfcontrol [*sic*] and a deeply religious bent. They could be of great service to India in her present transition. But even a stray visitor will be struck by the amazing and deplorable waste of energy which daily takes place in those veritable castles of indolence, otherwise known as monasteries and mutts where these ascetics lead a life of torpor and satisfied and dreamful ease. But they are not to blame. They are slaves to a superstition. They sincerely believe that strenuous life is opposed to spiritual perfection.[110]

This searing comment has value for persons in monasteries and convents of any religious tradition. Monks and nuns who would enjoy life "outside the walls" are to be admired as heroes and heroines if they choose freely to follow their strict religious discipline. But when their choice is motivated by fear of an active life in the outside world, they deserve not admiration but pity. The former are slaves to truth who separate from their families and friends when such separation is necessary for the purpose of loving and serving a wider community. The latter are slaves to a superstition which Radhakrishnan identifies as the false belief that strenuous life is opposed to spiritual perfection.

In summary, this chapter has presented some recurring themes in Radhakrishnan's faith. He thinks religion is an autonomous form of experience which directs attention from the external to the internal He conceives religion as essentially personal and neither dogmatic nor ceremonial. He defines it as experience of or living contact with ultimate reality, contact which results in the remaking of one's self, the transforming of one's nature. Born in agony, religion is not a refuge from the world. Finally, he

110. "Religion and Life," 104.

supposes that religion is a matter of feeling, requiring an objective philosophy to be shared with others.

Three aspects of Radhakrishnan's faith are to be noted, beginning with his faith (1)—his basic attitude of conviction. The world rests on spirit, confesses Radhakrishnan, and there is an ultimate oneness of things. His faith (2) consists of symbols for expressing and communicating his attitude of conviction. *Brahman*, *Īśvara*, *Hiraṇyagarbha*, and *Virāṭ* are four primary symbols. Another, the phrase *Brahman-Ātman*, illustrates the tremendous power of symbols. It expresses his attitude of conviction that the larger environment is of the nature of one's own self. His faith (3) consists of his beliefs which state the nature of the case propositionally. *Aham brahmāsmi* (I am Brahman), *tat tvam asi* (That art thou), and the threefold discipline signified by *puruṣārtha*, *varṇa*, and *āśrama* are a few examples. Others include his beliefs in an Absolute spirit, mystic consciousness, *karma*, and *mokṣa*.

The unity of religions is a theme recurring often in Radhakrishnan's faith. He thinks that we should stick to religion and let religions go, that Hinduism has no fixed creed, that we are suffering from the disease of dogmatism, and that active tolerance will establish concord (*samavāya*) in all spheres of life.

Radhakrishnan's faith is that of a modernist who supposes that openness to novelty and loyalty to tradition are compatible. While he has great respect for tradition, he refuses to defend exhausted traditions, dead forms, and obsolete watchwords. Instead, he calls on India to rise up and smash the spell of tired traditions.

His views on ethics relate closely to his non-illusional *māyā* hermeneutics. One of Radhakrishnan's lifelong tasks was to correct the impression of Schweitzer and others in both the West and the East that *advaita vedānta* has no room for a world-affirming ethic. Radhakrishnan holds that ethical ideals should be rooted in the universal nature of things and that absolute rules and ethical principles like *ahiṃsā* (non-violence) should be related to particular situations. In his view, non-attachment to objects of the world is the spirit which should motivate all human action. He wants "to save the world" by transforming the environment, not adjusting to it. Finally he is convinced that there is an organic relation between religious spirit and active life in the world. With these philosophical background concepts and recurring religious themes in Sir Sarvepalli's thought, we now can turn directly to six meanings of the term *māyā*.

4

Six Meanings of Māyā

This chapter sets forth Sir Sarvepalli Radhakrishnan's answer to the question "What is the meaning of *māyā*?" Etymologically, the term *māyā* is derived from the Sanskrit verbal root *mā* which means: (1) measure; (2) measure with, compare ; (3) mete out; (4) arrange, form; build; make.[1] Therefore, the literal meaning of *māyā* is "that which measures, arranges, forms, builds, makes." Whitney says the primary meaning of √mā is "to measure."[2] L.Thomas O'Neil agrees[3] in his helpful exposition of the ways and contexts in which *māyā* is used in the Rigvedic tradition. Radhakrishnan writes: "Māyā is that which measures out, moulds forms in the formless."[4] Unfortunately, the etymological meaning of *māyā* is only the tip of the proverbial iceberg. Most meanings of *māyā* in Radhakrishnan do not meet the etymological eye.

Radhakrishnan summarizes the meanings of *māyā* five times : *Indian Philosophy*, volume one, pages 546-547 (appendix I); *Indian Philosophy*, volume two, pages 573-574 (appendix II); *The Bhagavadgitā*, pages 42-43 (appendix III); *History of Philosophy Eastern and Western*, volume one, page 279 (appendix IV); and Paul Arthur Schilpp, ed., *The Philosophy of Sarvepalli Radhakrishnan*,

1. Charles Rockwell Lanman, *A Sanskrit Reader* (Cambridge: Harvard University Press, 1920; reprinted, 1967), p. 215.

2. William Dwight Whitney, *The Roots, Verb-Forms, and Primary Derivatives of the Sanskrit Language* (Leipzig: Breitkopf and Härtel, 1885), p. 119.

3. In *Māyā in Śaṅkara : Measuring the Immeasurable* (Columbia, Missouri: South Asia Books; Delhi: Motilal Banarsidass, 1980), p. 35.

4. PU, 83.

pages 800-802 (appendix V). Each of these summaries contains six parts.[5] It is therefore reasonable to conclude that Radhakrishnan thinks the term *māyā* has six meanings. Unfortunately, he does not give exactly the same six meanings in each summary. The 1948 summary in appendix III is used in order to organize this analysis of Radhakrishnan's *māyā* hermeneutics.

The meanings of *māyā* in the *Śvetāśvatara Upaniṣad* are summarized by the philosophy professor in a discussion of Indian philosophy which includes this observation: "These different significations [of *māyā*] are not irreconcilable, though confusion will result if we do not carefully distinguish them."[6] Heeding his advice, it seems wise to use superscripts in order to distinguish carefully among Radhakrishnan's six meanings of *māyā*. The overall thesis of this study is that as a Hindu modernist, Sarvepalli Radhakrishnan rejects an interpretation of *māyā* which says that the world is an illusion and accepts an interpretation which says that *māyā* has these six meanings: *māyā*^{1} as inexplicable mystery, *māyā*^{2} as power of self-becoming, *māyā*^{3} as duality of consciousness and matter, *māyā*^{4} as primal matter, *māyā*^{5} as concealment, and *māyā*^{6} as one-sided dependence.

I. Māyā as Inexplicable Mystery

Radhakrishnan is convinced that reality in its entirety cannot be grasped by the discursive intellect. This conviction shapes his first meaning of *māyā*. Philosophically speaking, *māyā*^{1} is epistemological, not ontological. Religiously speaking, *māyā*^{1} states Radhakrishnan's belief that mystery resides at the heart of things. Placing his epistemological conviction and his religious belief under one umbrella, we get *māyā*^{1} as inexplicable mystery. Most often, *māyā*^{1} signifies the inexplicable mystery surrounding the relation between Brahman and the world. Now and then it signifies other inexplicable mysteries, for instance:

> It is one thing to say that the secret of existence, how the unchangeable reality expresses itself in the changing universe,

5. The parts are numbered one through six in the first four summaries. The fifth summary is divided into four sections. Two of these sections have two parts.

6. IP, I, 513.

> without forfeiting its nature, is a mystery, and another to dismiss the whole changing universe as a mere mirage.[7]

When the unchangeable reality expresses itself in the changing universe, in Radhakrishnan's view, the result is not a *mere mirage*. *Mystery* and *mirage* do not have identical meanings. *Māyā*[1] does *not* indicate that the world is an illusion. This section describes Radhakrishnan's meaning of *māyā*[1] in four parts: (a) statements from summaries in the appendices; (b) the inexplicability of the relation between Brahman and the world ; (c) the idea that we are bound Prometheus-like to the rock of mystery; and (d) Radhakrishnan's recommendation that we adopt an attitude of wise agnosticism.

First, statements found in the appendices pertaining to *māyā*[1] are examined. Radhakrishnan uses the phrase "inexplicable mystery" in his 1948 summary: "If the Supreme Reality is unaffected by the events of the world then the rise of these events becomes an inexplicable mystery." (appendix III) It is significant that when Radhakrishnan wrote the "Introduction" to his translation of *The Bhagavadgitā* in 1948, he used virtually the same summary of the meanings of *māyā* which he had already published in 1923. (appendix I).

In his summary of the meanings of *māyā* in *advaita vedānta* philosophy (1927), Radhakrishnan employs the epistemological word "incomprehensibility":

> We can never understand how the ultimate reality is related to the world of plurality, since the two are heterogeneous, and every attempt at explanation is bound to fail. This incomprehensibility is brought out by the term *māyā*. (appendix II).

His 1952 summary (appendix IV) is virtually identical with his 1927 summary. In both, the relation between "the ultimate reality" and "the world of plurality" parallels the relation between poise one (Brahman) and poise four (*Virāṭ*), a relation which Radhakrishnan declares is logically inexplicable.

The reader is alerted that the second part of this section on *māyā*[1] has already begun. In a "Reply to Critics" published in

7. IP, II, 463.

The Philosophy of Sarvepalli Radhakrishnan, edited by Paul Arthur Schilpp, Radhakrishnan summarizes his interpretation of the status of the world and the doctrine of *māyā*, explaining:

> When the Absolute is taken as pure being, its relation to the world is inexplicable, *anirvacanīya*. We know that without the background of being there can be no world. The relation between the two cannot be logically explicated. This inexplicability of the logical relationship does not repudiate the existence of the world. It does not say that the world is not, though it appears to be. (appendix V)

Two points are particularly noteworthy. First, he places *inexplicable* and *anirvacanīya* in apposition. *Anirvacanīya* is a Sanskrit compound containing $\sqrt{}$*vac* meaning "to speak" plus the negative prefix "a". It conveys the idea that something cannot be spoken. *Anirvacanīya* means inexpressible.[8] In the second place, Radhakrishnan thinks the inexplicability of the logical relationship between the Absolute and the world does not repudiate the existence of the world. He asserts repeatedly that the world exists even though we cannot say exactly how. For instance, he confesses that "We do not and cannot know the why of this world. It is this fact of its inexplicable existence that is signified by the word *māyā*."[9] Primarily, *māyā*[1] as inexplicable mystery refers to the relation between Brahman and the world.

However, *māyā*[1] now and then signifies other kinds of mystery. For instance, Radhakrishnan agrees in part with Gauḍapāda and Śaṅkara that *māyā* signifies mystery in the relation between Ātman and the world:

> The word māyā is not used by Gauḍapāda with any strictness. It is used to indicate (1) the inexplicability of the relation between the Ātman and the world; (2) the nature or power of Iśvara; (3) the apparent dreamlike character of the world. The first is brought into greater prominence by Śaṁkara, who is indifferent to the third, which makes Gauḍapāda's posi-

8. HPEW, I, 280. Referring to the relation of the empirical world to Brahman, Radhakrishnan writes: "It is māyā, or mysterious, or anirvacanīya (inexplicable), as Śaṁkara puts it." (IP, I, 184). Cf. IP, II, 566, 638.

9. IP, I, 34.

tion more akin to the saṁvṛtisatya or untruth of the Mādhyamikas rather than to the vyāvahārikasatya or practical truth.[10] If Ātman and Brahman are identical, then the relation between Ātman and the world is identical with the relation between Brahman and the world. Elsewhere Radhakrishnan states that "this relation between the Ātman and the psychological self is inexplicable, māyā, or mysterious."[11] He thinks *māyā*[1] signifies mystery in the relation between the universal self (Ātman) and the particular self (ātman).

So far *māyā*[1] has been described as the inexplicability of the relation between Brahman and the world and between Ātman and ātman. Basically, *māyā*[1] in the writings of Sarvepalli Radhakrishnan signifies the inexplicability of *any* relation. He writes: "The inexplicability of the relation between the two is assumed by the Upaniṣads, and the later Vedānta gives to it the name of māyā."[12] *It* refers to *inexplicability.* What does Radhakrishnan mean by "the relation between the two?" The paragraph in which he makes this statement contains references to several pairs: God and the world, self-conscious Īśvara and indeterminate matter, Brahman on the one hand and subject and object on the other. The paragraph also contains Radhakrishnan's assertion that "The real is one, yet we have the two." It is reasonable to conclude that Radhakrishnan has in mind not only the relation between the specific relata to which he refers but also the relation between *any* "two." *Māyā*[1] as the inexplicability of *any* relation between *any* two is a facet of Radhakrishnan's monism. The concept of *māyā*[1] is coherent with his view that there is an ultimate oneness of things which dissolves all relations and relata.

In the third place, Radhakrishnan thinks we are "bound Prometheus-like to the rock of mystery by the chains of our finite mind."[13] *Māyā*[1] expresses this epistemological view. There are many passages in which Radhakrishnan uses *mystery* and *māyā* inter-changeably and they all illustrate *māyā*[1]. For instance, Radhakrishnan thinks "the transformation of the absolute into

10. IP, II, 461.
11. IP, II, 604.
12. IP, I, 186. The same point is made in IP, I, 538.
13. IP, II, 767.

God is māyā or a mystery."[14] He agrees with Śaṅkara: "If we raise the question as to how the finite rises from out of the bosom of the infinite, Śaṁkara says that it is an incomprehensible mystery, *māyā*."[15] Radhakrishnan comments on *Bhagavadgitā* IV.6 with its implications for the *avatāra* theory: "The assumption of imperfection by perfection, of lowliness by majesty, of weakness by power is the mystery of the universe. It is māyā from the logical standpoint."[16] Still elsewhere he says: "As to how the primal reality in which the divine light shines everlastingly can yet be the source and fount of all empirical being, we can only say that it is a mystery, māyā."[17] Finally, Radhakrishnan writes:

> As to why the divine should have permitted this particular plan, we can understand it when we cross the barrier of our limited intelligence, and see things from the Supreme Identity that lies behind the terrestrial process. From where we are, we can only say that it is a mystery (māyā), or is the divine will, or the expression of his creative force. Māyā does not mean that the world is a vain illusion, mere smoke without fire.[18]

Clearly, Radhakrishnan uses *māyā*[1] to signify mystery. He also denies that *māyā*[1] means the world is a vain illusion, a denial which is further evidence for the general thesis of this book.

Finally, Radhakrishnan recommends an attitude of wise agnosticism regarding cosmogonic questions. At the Sixth International Congress of Philosophy (1926) in Cambridge, Massachusetts, Radhakrishnan presented a paper entitled "The Doctrine of *Māyā*: Some Problems" which concludes:

> The most modest course for philosophers would be to admit a mystery at the center of things. Ko Veda......Kuta iyam visṛṣṭiḥ? Who knows whence this creation is born. It is māyā, mystery. Let us hold fast both ends and not try to

14. IP, I, 539.
15. HVL, 48.
16. BG, 154. Cf. IP, I, 544.
17. ERWT, 90.
18. RS, 104. Cf. the well-known passage: "As to why there is realisation of this possibility, we can only say that it is much too difficult for us in the pit to know what is happening behind the screens. It is māya [*sic*], or a mystery which we have to accept reverently." (IVL, 344)

> find out where the lines meet. The real is the supreme spirit; the actual multiplicity is rooted in the real. How, we do not know. It is a mystery which we cannot penetrate and a wise agnosticism is the only rational attitude.[19]

Admitting that there is mystery surrounding the origin of the universe is not the same as reveling in mystery for its own sake. Radhakrishnan does not begin with mystery; he ends there after serious attempts to investigate things rationally. He does not enjoy wallowing in the muck and mire of irrationality. As a modernist, he trusts reason; as a traditionalist, he trusts the past experience of *rishis* who affirm a mystery at the center of things. Radhakrishnan suggests that "the word 'māyā' registers our finiteness and points to a gap in our knowledge."[20] Elsewhere he admits candidly and therefore admirably that "We conceal our ignorance by the use of the word māyā."[21] Clearly, Radhakrishnan uses the concept of *māyā* to express his judgment that we do not know how to answer some of our most persistent questions. This meaning of *māyā* in the writings of Sarvepalli Radhakrishnan is confirmed by two secondary sources. Charles A. Moore reports: "Radhakrishnan insists repeatedly that we cannot answer the question 'Why?' and that the concept of *māyā* expresses this ultimate mystery."[22] Vishwanath S. Naravane explains that "There is another aspect of the doctrine of *Maya* to which Radhakrishnan has often drawn attention. This is the aspect of mystery which appeals to the poetic and imaginative side of human nature."[23]

To summarize this section, *māyā*[1] as inexplicable mystery is an epistemological concept which conveys Radhakrishnan's position that we cannot explain the relation between Brahman and the

19. E. S. Brightman, ed., *Proceedings of the Sixth International Congress of Philosophy* (New York: Longmans, Green and Company, 1927), p. 688. On "*ko veda* ?" and *māyā*, see IP, I, 102. On the phrase "wise agnosticism," see HVL, 49-50; IP, II, 658.

20. IP, II, 569.

21. IP, I, 538.

22. Charles A. Moore, "Metaphysics and Ethics in Radhakrishnan's Philosophy," in Paul Arthur Schilpp, ed., *The Philosophy of Sarvepalli Radhakrishnan* (New York: Tudor Publishing Company, 1952), p. 302.

23. Vishwanath S. Naravane, *Modern Indian Thought* (New York: Asia Publishing House, 1964), p. 248.

world. He portrays this relation as inexpressible (*anirvacanīya*). Basically, *māyā*[1] in Radhakrishnan's hermeneutics signifies the inexplicability of *any* relation. He thinks we are bound Prometheus-like to the rock of mystery by the chains of our finite minds. Using the words *māyā* and *mystery* interchangeably, Radhakrishnan recommends that we maintain an attitude of wise agnosticism regarding the ultimate cosmogonic questions.

II. Māyā[2] as Power of Self-Becoming

Radhakrishnan's writings contain six meanings of *māyā*, none of which is closer to the etymological meaning of the term than *māyā*[2]. Etymologically, the word *māyā* means that which measures, arranges, forms, builds, makes. As the power of self-becoming, *māyā*[2] is that which measures out, molding forms in the formless. *Māyā*[2] is closely related to theories of creation. Whereas *māyā*[1] is an epistemological concept, *māyā*[2] is a cosmogonic concept. It refers to the creative activity which Radhakrishnan identifies as poise two of reality—Īśvara. This section considers: (1) statements of *māyā*[2] in the appendices; (2) the power of self-becoming as the power of self-expression; (3) the power of self-becoming as the power of creation; and (4) *māyā*[2] as it relates to the theory of illusion.

Statements of *māyā*[2] in the appendices refer to "the power of self-becoming" (appendices I and III), "the power of self-expression (appendices II and IV), "creative power" (appendix V), and "the power of manifestation" (appendix V). Radhakrishnan uses all of these phrases to invite our attention to that which he calls *māyā* and which we call *māyā*.[2]

"The power of self-becoming" is Radhakrishnan's translation of *ātmavibhūti*, a compound of *ātman* and √*bhū* plus *vi*. Ātman cannot be translated into English adequately, but it is often rendered *self*.[24] Monier-Williams says the prefix *vi* plus the verbal root *bhū* in the *Ṛg Veda* means "to arise, be developed or manifested, expand, appear." Therefore, *ātmavibhūti* means" the arising, developing, manifesting, expanding, or appearing of the

24. Monier-Williams says ātman is variously derived from √*an*, to breathe; √at, to move; √va, to blow. He says *ātman* in the *Ṛg Veda* means "the breath; the soul, the principle of life and sensation."

self." Two points about this self are noteworthy. First, the absolute self (*Ātman*) in Radhakrishnan's view is "that one."[25] Therefore, *māyā*[2] as a philosophical concept refers to the power of "that one" to become the many. Radhakrishnan and Plotinus both put forth theories of emanation. Second, Radhakrishnan views the absolute self (Ātman) as Brahman. Therefore, *māyā*[2] as a religious symbol expresses his attitude of conviction that Brahman becomes the world. Earlier it was noted that Radhakrishnan derives *Brahman* from $\sqrt{}$*bṛh* meaning to grow, to burst forth. He is convinced that the world is the result of the "growth" or the "bursting forth" which is Brahman.

It is important to notice that Radhakrishnan's theory of self-becoming is not like theories of creation familiar to students of the Bible and the Qur'an. These theories of creation posit an *independent* deity which causes the world to come into being. But Radhakrishnan's theory of self-becoming posits no such independent deity. While Radhakrishnan contends that Īśvara, with respect to *Hiraṇyagarbha* (the world-soul) and *Virāṭ* (the world), is completely independent, he also contends that Īśvara with respect to Brahman is *not* independent. Without Brahman, Īśvara would be cosmogonically impotent.

Māyā in the writings of S. Radhakrishnan sometimes refers to the "power of self-expression." The category *māyā*[2] is intended to include all such references. Radhakrishnan reports that "The power of self-expression possessed by the personal Ishvara (God) is sometimes called maya."[26] Elsewhere he writes: "The absolute is looked upon as a personal God by whose power of self-expression or māyā the world is sustained."[27] He states clearly:

> Theoretical philosophy, interested in deducing the world of being from the first principle of an absolute self which has nothing contingent about it, is obliged, whether in East or West, to accept some principle of self-expression (māyā), of objectivity (prakṛti)....The self limitation of the primal consciousness, or the rise of the obstacle against which the

25. Cf. *tadekam* (*Ṛg Veda* X. 129)

26. *Encyclopedia Britannica*, 14th ed., s.v. "Indian Philosophy," by S. Radhakrishnan.

27. IP, I, 675.

> self breaks itself, has to be assumed, however incomprehensible it may be. Similarly in the conception of Iśvara we have, besides the absolute Brahman, the element of objectivity or prakṛti, self-expression or māyā.[28]

Radhakrishnan thinks that an absolute self (Ātman) requires the power of self-expression in order to produce the world. He reasons that primal consciousness must have the capacity to limit itself, to break itself into the objects of the world. He refers to "the self-sundering of the Eternal which calls into existence the universe of men and things"[29] and reports that "this self-limiting power of the Absolute is called in Indian philosophy *Māyā*."[30] Radhakrishnan composes several other variations on this theme, for instance: "Māyā represents at the conceptual level the self-distinction residing in the very heart of reality, propelling it to develop itself."[31] Another variation illustrates the close connection between *māyā*^{2} and the etymological meaning of *māyā* : "Māyā is used as the name of the dividing force, the finitising principle, that which measures out the immeasurable and creates forms in the formless."[32] In short, *māyā*^{2} as the power of self-becoming is also described by Radhakrishnan as the power of self-expression, the self-sundering of the Eternal the self-limiting power of the Absolute, the self-distinction residing in the very heart of reality, the dividing force, and the finitising principle.

It is important to notice that Radhakrishnan thinks this power of self-expression is a *sine qua non* of the Absolute. There is a well-known song which children sing : "My hat, it has three corners; three corners has my hat. And had it not three corners, it would not be my hat." These lyrics illustrate the certitude which results from a circular argument. Now consider Radhakrishnan's claim: "Māyā is the objectifying or manifesting tendency. If the power

28. IP, II, 554-555. Cf. HVL, 50. Radhakrishnan also says *māyā* is "the force of self-expression." (IP, II, 609)

29. PRT, 28.

30. RRCP, 164. He cites with approval what he calls the Hegelian phraseology: "the self separates itself from itself to return to itself to be itself." (RRCP, 444)

31. IP, I, 197. Cf. "Māyā, in the sense of energy, is potentially eternal in being." (IP, I, 186)

32. IP, II, 570. Cf. Radhakrishnan's reference to a "principle of māyā or svabhāva." (IP, II, 460)

of manifestation were excluded from the nature of the Absolute, it would not be the Absolute."[33] *Māyā*² is this objectifying tendency, this power of manifestation.

It is also important to notice Radhakrishnan's view that the objectification or manifestation of the Absolute does not affect its unity or integrity. He reports that:

> This power of actualisation is given the name of *māyā* in later Vedānta, for the manifestation does not distrub the unity and integrity of the One. The One becomes manifested by its own intrinsic power, by its *tapas*.[34]

Radhakrishnan's view is that the ultimate oneness of things is not shattered when *māyā*² objectifies that which was previously beyond the duality of subject and object. Neither is it shattered when *māyā*² actualizes that which was previously pure potential or manifests that which was previously unmanifested.[35]

So far in this section the reader's attention has been invited to statements of *māyā*² in the appendices and *māyā*² as the power of self-expression. *Māyā*² as the power of creation is the next item for consideration. *Creation* is the standard translation of the Sanskrit word *sṛṣṭi*. However, Radhakrishnan points out quite correctly that "The Sanskrit word *sṛṣṭi* means literally emanation, letting loose"[36] and adds elsewhere that "The theory of emanation is distinguished from creation."[37] It is important to keep in mind the distinction between emanation theories and creation theories. Emanation theories state that the many emanate from

33. RCW, 87-88.

34. PU, 35-36. Cf. "The world is the play of *Brahman*, his *vilāsa*, his *māyā*. It is the expression of the urge in *Brahman* to become many." (BS, 36) Cf. also Radhakrishnan's sermon "Chaos and Creation," delivered at Manchester College, Oxford, November, 1929, in which he compares *tapas* with the brooding or moving of the spirit upon the face of the waters as described in Genesis I.2 (EWR, 73-98).

35. Cf. "As the Supreme brings forth the whole universe by His own power of māyā, He is not in any way affected by it as others are." (PU, 734) See ERWT, 92. This is the meaning of the concept *māyā*⁶ which is presented later in this study.

36. BS, 140. Cf. "If we are earnest students of truth (*paramārthacintakāḥ*) and not mere speculators about creation (*sṛṣṭicintakāḥ*), we shall see that there is no such thing as creation at all." (IP, II, 459)

37. ERWT, 210.

the one without ever really separating themselves from the one whereas creation theories state that there is a real separation between the creator and the created. Radhakrishnan's theory that the self becomes the universe of plurality and individuality is a theory of emanation in that he thinks there is no real separation between the many and the one. Such a real separation is precluded by his view of the ultimate oneness of things. In order to explain his interpretation of *māyā* to Western audiences, Radhakrishnan often refers to *māyā* as the power of creation. These references give the impression that Radhakrishnan's cosmogonic theory is a theory of creation. This is a false impression because he does not think there is any real separation between the creator and the created, *Īśvara* and *Virāṭ*, respectively. In the final analysis, he thinks they are poises of one reality.

Without a doubt, Radhakrishnan thinks that *māyā* is the power of creation[38] (*sṛṣṭi*) and that this power of creation is Īśvara's. Many passages illustrate Radhakrishnan's use of the word *māyā* in this way such as his claim that "the world is created by the power of māyā of Īśvara."[39] Radhakrishnan indicates that the meaning of *māyā* as creative power is the meaning contained in the *Ṛg Veda* :

> The *Śvetāśvatara Upaniṣad* describes God as *māyin*, the wonder-working powerful Being, who creates the world by His powers. Here *māyā* is used in the sense in which the *Ṛg Veda* employs it, the divine art or power by which the divinity makes a likeness of the eternal prototypes or ideas inherent in his nature. Indra is declared to have assumed many shapes by his māyā. Māyā is the power of *Īśvara* from which the world arises.[40]

38. PU, 90.

39. PU, 87. Cf. BS, 30.

40. PU, 82-83. Cf. "God, the self-conscious Īśvara, is the great *māyin* who produces the world." (ERWT, 92) Cf. also his references to a "God who with His protean magic or māyā shapes and reshapes for ever all cosmic being." (IP, I, 459) Also see IP, II, 460.

Radhakrishnan thinks God as *māyin* makes likenesses of the eternal prototypes or ideas inherent in his nature. In his view, these likenesses constitute the world. It is important to note in this connection that nothing in the concept *likeness* necessarily implies *illusion* or *mirage*. When an artist makes a likeness of someone, no one rushes to the conclusion that the sculpted bust or painted portrait is an illusion or a mirage.

Furthermore, Radhakrishnan describes *māyā* as creative energy. These descriptions illustrate *māyā*², for instance: "Māyā is the energy of Īśvara, his inherent force, by which he transforms the potential into the actual world."[41] He identifies this creative energy of Īśvara as *śakti*: "*māyā* denotes the śakti, or the energy of Īśvara."[42] That Radhakrishnan's cosmogonic writings contain a theory of emanation is confirmed in another passage which relates *māyā*² and *śakti*:

> God has the power to become anything at any time through what is known as his *māyā-śakti*. He is the creator of everything and is the material and efficient cause of the world. God does not create by using *prakṛti* but through his own nature.[43]

Remarkably, Radhakrishnan describes Īśvara as both the material and the efficient cause of the world. Īśvara is not the efficient cause which brings about the world out of something else, in Radhakrishnan's view. He thinks Īśvara brings about the world by becoming it, not by creating it. He consistently denies a dualism of God and something else. This discussion has now come full circle from Radhakrishnan's view that *māyā*² is the power of creation to his view that *māyā*² is the power of self-becoming (*ātmavibhūti*).

Finally, Radhakrishnan's conception of *māyā*² in no way supports the theory that the world is an illusion. He does not think the power of creation is a power of illusion, writing early in his career that:

> The accounts of creation in the Upanishads are not to be taken seriously; but they clearly show that the Upanishad

41. IP, II, 572.
42. Ibid., 571. Cf. HPEW, I, 277; BS, 36, 71, 127, 141.
43. BS, 90. Cf. IP, II, 549.

> writers did not conceive the world as pure illusion. They regarded the world as real and seriously set about accounting for its reality.[44]

Radhakrishnan's argument rests on a reasonable assumption. Writers who are their own final authority do not write about the creation of the world if they think the world is an illusion. In the following passage, Radhakrishnan uses the phrase "Maya doctrine" to indicate the doctrine of *māyā* which states that the nature of the world is illusory: "If the Maya doctrine had really been held by the earlier Vedantins, they would have said something about Maya when the theories of creation were described."[45] The phrase "the doctrine of *māyā*" at the end of the following passage is used in the same way:

> When the *Śvetāśvatara Upaniṣad* looks upon the Supreme as the great Māyin, it suggests that this wonderful creation is his product. The Upaniṣads do not support the view that the Supreme calls up appearances which have no existence except in deluded minds. The different theistic systems adopted by the large majority of the Hindus do not advocate the doctrine of *māyā*.[46]

Radhakrishnan's use of the phrase "wonderful creation" is significant because it indicates a positive attitude toward the created world. This positive attitude of conviction is as important as the symbols Radhakrishnan uses to express it and the beliefs he uses to state it. In his "Introduction" to his translation of *The Bhagavadgītā*, Radhakrishnan states :

> The creative power by which God fashions the universe is called *yoga māyā*. There is no suggestion that the forms, the events and the objects produced by māyā or the form-building power of God, the māyin, are only illusory.[47]

44. "The VP and the DM," p. 437. Cf. "We see clearly that there is no basis for any conception of the unreality of the world in the hymns of the Ṛg-veda. The world is not a purposeless phantasm, but is just the evolution of God. Wherever the word māyā occurs, it is used only to signify the might or the power: 'Indra takes many shapes quickly by his māyā'." (IP, I, 103)

45. Ibid., p. 447.

46. HVL, 45.

47. BG, 41. Cf. "God manifests himself as many through *māyā*. The manifestation is not an error or illusion." (BS, 91)

Māyā as the form-building power of God is *māyā*². *Māyā*² in the writings of S. Radhakrishnan is a cosmogonic concept which lends no support to the theory that the world is an illusion.

To summarize this section on *māyā*² as the power of self-becoming, the meaning of *māyā*² is closely related to the etymological meaning of *māyā*. *Māyā*² is a cosmogonic concept. The phrase "power of self-becoming" is Radhakrishnan's translation of *ātma-vibhūti*. Radhakrishnan's theory of self-becoming is unlike Biblical or Qur'anic creation theories because it has no concept of an independent deity which creates something separate. *Māyā*² also means the power of self-expression. Radhakrishnan asserts that without this power of self-expression, the Absolute would not be the Absolute. He contends that the self-manifestation of the Absolute does not affect its unity or integrity. *Māyā*² also means the power of creation if creation is meant as a translation of *sṛṣṭi*. Even though Radhakrishnan often refers to a creative power, his cosmogonic theory is actually a theory of emanation. He describes the power of creation (*sṛṣṭi*) as Īśvara's. He portrays *māyā* as creative energy (*śakti*). Finally, Radhakrishnan argues that *māyā*² as the power of self-becoming does not support the theory that the world is an illusion.

III. Māyā³ as Duality of Consciousness and Matter

*Māyā*¹ as inexplicable mystery is an epistemological concept and *māyā*² as power of self-becoming is a cosmogonic concept. *Māyā*³ as duality of consciousness (*puruṣa*) and matter (*prakṛti*) is a "uniting" concept. Radhakrishnan uses *māyā*³ to unite the Sāṁkhya and Vedānta *darśanas*. Just as he used the concept of absolute idealism in *The Reign of Religion in Contemporary Philosophy* to unite the philosophies of Bergson, Russell and others with his own Vedānta philosophy, Radhakrishnan uses *māyā*³ to unite Sāṁkhya thought with his own point of view. He incorporates the Sāṁkhya categories *puruṣa* (consciousness) and *prakṛti* (matter) into his own system. Radhakrishnan's system is *advaita vedānta*, a system in which non-duality is ultimately real. He thinks the duality of consciousness and matter is only penultimately real.

Radhakrishnan's published works contain less direct evidence for *māyā*³ than for any other meanings of *māyā*. Nevertheless, there is some evidence that he thinks *māyā* signifies the duality of consciousness and matter: "Since the Lord is able to produce the universe by means of the two elements of His being, prakṛti and puruṣa, matter and consciousness, they are said to be māyā (higher and lower) of God." (appendix III) This is Radhakrishnan's only reference to "higher and lower" *māyā*. The uniqueness of the phrase prevents us from checking its meaning in another context. It is difficult to imagine why he did not write "lower and higher" since he values prakṛti (matter) less than puruṣa (consciousness). The phrasing may be a simple oversight. In any case, *māyā*[3] is not intended primarily to signify the relative values which Radhakrishnan assigns to matter and consciousness.

Māyā[3] is intended to signify "the two elements of His [Īśvara's] being." *Māyā*[3] calls attention to Radhakrishnan's view that *twoness* or *duality* of consciousness and matter, being and non-being, is inherent in all things. He remarks that "All things partake of the duality of being and non-being from Puruṣottama downwards. Even God has the element of negativity or māyā though He controls it."[48] Puruṣottama is Īśvara, poise two of reality. Radhakrishnan thinks even Īśvara's nature is dual. However, *māyā*[3] is intended to call attention to the duality of consciousness and matter in "all things." Radhakrishnan holds that the world process is dual: a mixture of self and not-self, spirit and nature, consciousness and matter:

> If we turn to the world process which is a perpetual becoming it is a mixture of being and non-being, *sat* and *asat*, the divine principle and *prakṛti*. *Hiraṇya-garbha* and his world are both subject to time, and should be distinguished from the eternal. But the temporal becoming is by no means false.[49]

It is important to notice that Radhakrishnan couples *the divine principle* and *prakṛti*. The Sāṁkhya duality between *puruṣa* and *prakṛti* is just below the surface. It is also important to notice that Radhakrishnan couples *Hiraṇya-garbha* and *his world*. The context indicates that he has in mind *Hiraṇyagarbha* (the world-spirit) and *Virāṭ* (the world). In short, *Hiraṇyagarbha* (poise three) and *Virāṭ* (poise four) express symbolically the duality of con-

48. BG, 27.
49. PU, 90.

sciousness and matter which Radhakrishnan thinks is inherent in all things and even in Īśvara.

There is direct evidence for *māyā*³ as duality of consciousness and matter in a paragraph which comprises section III of appendix V. The paragraph begins: "In the world process itself, we have the divine interacting with primal matter." The paragraph ends:

> All things in the world participate in the characters of this duality. They are *sad-asad-ātmaka*. They are real as well as unreal. This dual character is sometimes indicated by the word *māyā*. The world and the World Spirit are both equally real. (appendix V)

This *dual character* is indicated by *māyā*³. It is important to notice that Radhakrishnan mentions the world (*Virāṭ*) and the World Spirit (*Hiraṇyagarbha*) in the context of *māyā*³ to express symbolically the inherent duality of consciousness and matter in all things. He cites with approval a statement from the *Vedāntasāra*: "The world of duality is mere māyā, the real being the non-dual."[50]

*Māyā*³ is like an ellipse. An ellipse is the locus of all points the sum of whose distances from two fixed points is equal. Usually oval, an ellipse can be drawn by tying a string loosely between two nails, by pulling the string taut with a pencil point, and by swinging the pencil all the way around the two nails. The two nails in this simile are consciousness and matter. All things in the universe lie somewhere on the ellipse itself. They are all comprised of consciousness and matter to some degree. *Māyā*³ signifies this duality inherent in all things.

To summarize this brief section on *māyā*³ as duality of consciousness and matter, Radhakrishnan uses *māyā*³ to unite the Sāṁkhya and Vedānta *darśanas*. There is less direct evidence for this meaning of *māyā* than for the other five meanings. *Māyā*³ calls attention to Radhakrishnan's view that *twoness* or *duality* is inherent in all things, a worldview suggested by an ellipse.

50. IP, II, 460.

IV. Māyā[4] as Primal Matter

In his "Introduction" to his translation of *The Bhagavadgītā*, Radhakrishnan indicates that "We may here distinguish the different senses in which the word 'māyā' is used and indicate its place in the *Gītā*." (appendix III) He then states the six meanings of *māyā* being used as the model for this study. The statement includes: "(4) Gradually, māyā comes to mean the lower prakṛti, since puruṣa is said to be the seed which the Lord casts into the womb of prakṛti for the generation of the universe." (appendix III) Just as *māyā*[3] is a concept used by Radhakrishnan to unite the Sāṁkhya and Vedānta philosophies, so also does *māyā*[4] unite Sāṁkhya and Vedānta. For instance, Sāṁkhya cosmogony is reflected in Radhakrishnan's statement that the seed of consciousness enters the womb of matter for the generation of the universe.

For Radhakrishnan, the phrase "primal matter" is identical with the phrases "lower *prakṛti*" and "unmanifested *prakṛti*." For example, he proclaims that "In the world process itself, we have the divine interacting with primal matter, what Indian thinkers call the unmanifested *prakṛti*. This is also called *māyā*." (appendix V) Elsewhere he explains that "Sometimes *māyā* is said to be the primal matter or *prakṛti*."[51] The term *māyā*[4] refers to this meaning of *māyā*.

Māyā[4] as primal matter, in Radhakrishnan's view, is that from which all existence arises. He theorizes that "Māyā is also used for *prakṛti*, the objective principle which the personal God uses for creation."[52] The view that Īśvara (*Puruṣa*, the primal person) uses primal matter (*prakṛti*) for creating the world is consistent with some Sāṁkhya cosmogonic ideas. However, Radhakrishnan does not share the pluralistic Sāṁkhya view that *puruṣa* and *prakṛti* are independent:

> The world is traced to the development of *prakṛti* which is also called *māyā* in the Advaita Vedānta, but this *prakṛti* or *māyā* is not independent of spirit. It is dependent on Brahman. Brahman with *prakṛti* or *māyā* is *sa-guṇa* Brahman or

51. BS, 72.
52. PU, 86.

Īśvara comprehending the diversity of souls and objects.[53]

Radhakrishnan thinks that primal matter or *māyā*[4] is dependent on Brahman whereas Sāṁkhya dualism posits spirit and matter as separate and independent principles. Radhakrishnan agrees with the Sāṁkhya position that all existence arises from primal matter and that primal matter is not an illusion. But he disagrees with the Sāṁkhya position that Puruṣa is an independent deity, a separate creative power.

Even though Radhakrishnan interprets *māyā*[1] as inexplicable mystery which surrounds the relation between Brahman and the world, he remains curious, always searching for a theoretical explanation of how the one becomes the many—how Brahman becomes Virāṭ. It is particularly noteworthy that Radhakrishnan's emanation theory is stated in a way which is intended to unite Vedānta, Sāṁkhya, Vaishnavism and Shaivism:

> The Absolute breaks up its wholeness and develops the reality of self and not-self. The self is God, and the not-self the matter of the universe. All Hindu systems of philosophy posit these two ultimate principles. In the *Sankhya* it is *Purusha* and *Prakriti*; in the *Vedanta* it is *Iswara* and *Maya*; in *Vaishnavism* it is *Krishna* and *Radha*; and in *Shaivism* it is *Shiva* and *Shakti*. *Maya*, *Radha* and *Shakti* are respectively the intellectual, the emotional and the volitional aspects of *Prakriti*. *Krishna*, *Shiva* and *Iswara* are one in essence, and so are *Radha*, *Shakti* and *Maya*.[54]

Radhakrishnan uses the Sāṁkhya theory of the three guṇas—*sattva*, *rajas*, and *tamas*—to unite Maya, Radha, and Shakti. But he uses the Advaita Vedānta theory of the Absolute to unite Sāṁkhya dualism and his own non-dualism. He pictures the Absolute with its power of self-becoming—Brahman with its *māyā*[2]—bursting forth into the *self* and the *not-self*. Equating the self with God and the not-self with primal matter, he calls the

53. HPEW, I, 276. Cf. "The Sāṁkhya account is accepted with modifications. Prakṛti ceases to be an independent power, but becomes of the very nature of God." (IP, I, 513) Cf. also "If we think nature to be separate from God, we are in the world of *māyā*." (PRT, 68-69)

54. RRCP, 444. Cf. Radhakrishnan's reference to "the not-self or Prakriti or Maya." (PRT, 29)

primal matter *māyā*. Here it is being called *māyā*[4] in order to distinguish it from other meanings of *māyā*. It is important to note that Radhakrishnan does not think *māyā*[4] means illusion. Primal matter is fully real in so far as it is seen to be part of the whole.

Many other statements[55] by Radhakrishnan contain direct evidence that he uses the word *māyā* to mean *prakṛti*, primal matter. There is support for this interpretation of *māyā* in *Śvetāśvatara Upaniṣad* IV. 10a which he translates:

> Know then that *prakṛti is māyā*
> and the wielder of *māyā* is the Great Lord.[56]

R. C. Zaehner translates this passage in a way which makes the meaning of *māyā*[4] even clearer:

> *Māyā* is material Nature (*prakṛti*), this must be known,
> And He who possesses it is the Mighty Lord.[57]

Zaehner's *material Nature* is Radhakrishnan's *primal matter*. There can be no doubt that Radhakrishnan and others use the word *māyā* in the sense which we are identifying as *māyā*[4], primal matter.

To summarize the meaning of *māyā*[4], Radhakrishnan states in his "Introduction" to *The Bhagavadgitā* that *māyā* gradually came to mean lower *prakṛti*. He thinks the phrases *lower prakṛti* and *primal matter* are identical and that all existence arises from this primal matter. He tries to unite Sāṁkhya dualism and his own non-dualism by suggesting an emanation theory according to which the Absolute breaks up its wholeness and develops the duality of self and not-self. Sāṁkhya calls it a duality of Puruṣa and *prakṛti* while Vedānta calls it a duality of Īśvara and *māyā*. Radhakrishnan's use of the word *māyā* in this sense is what this section calls *māyā*[4], primal matter.

V. Māyā[5] as Concealment

Radhakrishnan's conviction that there is "something more"

55. IP, II, 260, 326, 549, 556, 557-558, 572-573, 588, 610, 612, 736, 761, 763; BS, 99.
56. PU, 734.
57. Robert Charles Zaehner, trans., *The Bhagavadgītā* (Oxford: Clarendon Press, 1969; Oxford paperback), p. 183. Cf. Zaehner's commentary on *The Bhagavadgītā* VII.14. (Ibid., p. 249)

behind the phenomena of nature and the drama of history has been noted in Chapter one. Chapter two set forth his definition of philosophy as a logical inquiry into the nature of reality. Chapter three presented his view that religion is contact with or immediate experience of reality (*anubhava*). This section of chapter four examines Sir Sarvepalli's view that phenomenal things conceal "something more" which is behind them. He contends that our logical inquiry into the nature of reality is blocked because the manifested world hides the unity and harmony of the whole:

> (5) As the manifested world hides the real from the vision of mortals, it is said to be delusive in character. The world is not an illusion, though by regarding it as a mere mechanical determination of nature unrelated to God, we fail to perceive its Divine essence. It then becomes a source of delusion....God seems to be enveloped in the immense cloak of māyā. (appendix III)

Radhakrishnan depicts the world as a source of delusion, not an illusion. The world deludes, he generalizes, when the perceiver fails to perceive it as it really is—related to God. The implication is that the problem of *māyā* is inherent in the attitude of those who perceive, not in that which is perceived.

The definitions of *illusion*, *delusion*, and *hallucination* must be considered carefully. First of all, an *illusion* is a distorted or abnormal perception. It is important to notice that the meaning of the term *illusion* extends over the entire range of perceptual psychology—physiological psychology as well as abnormal psychology. Discussion of "distorted" perceptions belongs in the realm of physiological psychology. An optical illusion is an example of a distorted perception. Secondly, a *delusion* is a persistent and false belief about one's self. *Delusion* is a term whose extension is limited to abnormal psychology. The term is improper in the realm of physiological psychology. A delusion of grandeur is an example of an abnormal perception. The term *illusion* is generic; the term *delusion* is specific. Finally, *hallucination* is perception of an object which does not exist in the perceiver's physical environment. A pink elephant in a psychiatric hospital room is an example of hallucination.

In the block quotation above, Radhakrishnan states that "the world is not an illusion." In other words, he does not think the world is a distorted or abnormal perception. He also says the world "becomes a source of delusion" when we consider it to be a mere mechanical determination of nature unrelated to God. In other words, he thinks the world can become the source of a persistent and false belief about one's self. He considers "normal" perception to be perception of the whole—the manifested world *and* "something more" behind it. He regards "abnormal" perception as perception of the parts alone—the manifested world and *nothing* more. He takes the position that in abnormal perception the world hides or conceals "something more." Radhakrishnan uses the word *māyā* to signify this "hiding." In his view, the word *māyā* signifies a "veiling," a "cloaking," a "concealment." Such concealment is the meaning of *māyā*^{5}. This section analyzes *māyā*^{5} in five parts: (a) as concealment; (b) as a source of delusion; (c) as a distortion of vision; (d) as an axiological concept; and (e) as ignorance (*avidyā*).

First of all, Radhakrishnan regards *māyā*^{5} as "the beginningless cosmic principle which hides reality from the vision of man."[58] He believes liberation (*mokṣa*) from endless rebirth (*saṁsāra*) requires a vision of the real. Since *māyā*^{5} blocks such a vision, it prevents liberation. *Māyā*^{5} is a soteriological concept, and its meaning for Radhakrishnan will be misunderstood if its soteriological context is forgotten. He is convinced that "māyā as concealment has no power over the liberated soul."[59] In other words, he regards what might be called "liberation power" as greater than "concealment power." *Māyā*^{2} as power of self-becoming and *māyā*^{5} as concealment are both illustrated in a statement by Radhakrishnan which includes a quotation from Browning:

> Māyā evolves a variety of names and forms, which in their totality is the jagat or the universe. It also conceals the eternal Brahman under this aggregate of names and forms. Māyā has the two functions of concealment of the real and the projection of the unreal. The world of variety screens us from the real.

58. IP, II, 460.
59. IP, II, 639.

Some think Creation's meant to show him forth,
I say it's meant to hide him all it can.
Browning, *Bishop Blougram's Apology*[60]

Clearly, Radhakrishnan thinks that one function of *māyā* is to conceal, to hide. His metaphorical affirmation that "God seems to be enveloped in the immense cloak of māyā" has already been noted and the function of a cloak is to cover. Radhakrishnan also refers to "the veil of māyā."[61] He modifies the veil metaphor in a particularly noteworthy passage: "In Hindu thought, *māyā* is not so much a veil as the dress of God."[62] A dress serves two purposes—it hides *and* it displays. Likewise, *māyā*^{5} can be likened to a scrim. A scrim is used in theater and opera in order both to show the audience shapes and colors and to hide what is going on backstage.

Secondly, Radhakrishnan interprets *māyā*^{5} as the source of delusion.[63] It has been noted that a delusion is a persistent and false belief about one's self. In other words, Radhakrishnan thinks that *māyā*^{5} is the source of a persistent and false belief about the human self. The persistent and false belief about the self, in his view, is the belief that the true self (*Ātman*) is the same as the apparent self (*ātman*): "*Māyā* is a term employed also to indicate the tendency to identify ourselves with our apparent selves."[64] In a word, Radhakrishnan supposes that humankind suffers from "delusions of individuality." While the phrase is not his, it states the meaning of *māyā*^{5}. He theorizes that "The individuals are subject to māyā, or delusion, being lost in outer appearances....We get rid of individuality when we transcend māyā and realise our true status."[65] He recommends that the way to transcend *māyā*^{5} and realize the self's true status is to share his faith (1) in the ultimate oneness of all things including selves:

60. IP, II, 571. Cf. Radhakrishnan's quotation from *Prakaṭārthavivaraṇa*: "māyā which is possessed of the two powers of enveloping and projecting." (IP, II, 609)

61. ERWT, 94; BS, 35.

62. BS, 156-157.

63. See BG, 41, 218.

64. WUS, 25.

65. IP, I, 549-550. Cf. IP, I, 192.

> The view which regards the multiplicity as ultimate is deceptive (*māyā*), for it causes the desire to live separate and independent lives. When we are under the influence of *māyā*, we think we are completely separate entities, sharing little and mistaking individuality, which is one of the conditions of our life in space-time, for isolation and not wishing to lose the hard outlines of our separate existence. *Māyā* keeps us busy with the world of succession and finitude.[66]

Radhakrishnan deems it necessary to erase the hard outline of separate existence. In a discussion of Śāktism Radhakrishnan makes this statement about the individual self (*jīva*): "The jīva, under the influence of māyā, looks upon itself as an independent agent and enjoyer until release is gained."[67] There is additional evidence that Radhakrishnan's *māyā* hermeneutics includes *māyā*[5] as the source of "delusions of individuality":

> So long as the individual thinks himself to be a separate atom in this immense universe, so long as the feeling of isolation has him by the throat, so long as he has the idea that he is the chief actor in the stage, he is in the world of Maya,... When we recognize the essence of the finite to be in the Infinite, when we realise that we are parts of a stupendous whole, when we know that we are but the instruments of a nobler purpose, we get out of the world of Maya.[68]

The recurring theme *that art thou* (*tat tvam asi*) in Radhakrishnan's faith (3) is reflected in the clause "When we recognise the essence of the finite to be in the Infinite." The background concept of the whole in Radhakrishnan's ontology is reflected in the clause "when we realise that we are parts of a stupendous whole." It has been noted that Radhakrishnan's idealism posits ideas, ideals, or values conceived as operative creative forces. They are reflected in the clause "when we know that we are but the instruments of a nobler purpose." Quite naturally Radhakrishnan proposes ways of dispelling the false and persistent belief in individuality.

66. ERWT, 94.
67. IP, II, 736.
68. "Religion and Life." p. 100. Cf. The Maya theory simply says that we are under an illusion if we think that the world of individuals, the pluralistic universe of the intellect, is the absolute reality." (RRCP, 445)

To borrow a root image from Indian thought, it could be said that Radhakrishnan believes the delusive river of individual existence can be crossed in the soteriological vehicle (*yāna*) of his own philosophy and faith.

Borrowing a root image from Western thought, Radhakrishnan diagnoses the people in Plato's cave as suffering from the persistent and false belief that the shadows are the real:

> The simile of the cave reminds us of the Hindu doctrine of *māyā*, or appearance. Plato compares the human race to men sitting in a cave, bound, with their backs to the light and fancying that the shadows on the wall before them are not shadows but real objects.[69]

They suffer because they are prevented from seeing the whole, in Radhakrishnan's view. He cautions that "This world of *māyā* has thrown our consciousness out of focus"[70] and predicts that people are doomed to live in the cave forever if they do not bring their consciousness into focus. Continuing the photographic metaphor, Radhakrishnan urges people to adjust the lens of their mind's eye so as to focus on the parts *and* the whole. He wants people to expand their partial consciousness by seeing both the forms *and* the formless:

> Through the force of māyā we have a bewildering partial consciousness which loses sight of the reality and lives in the world of phenomena. God's real being is veiled by the play of prakṛti and its modes. The world is said to be deceptive because God hides Himself behind His creation. The world is not a deception but the occasion for it. We must shatter all forms, get behind the veil to find the reality. The world and its changes constitute the self-concealment of God (*tirodhāna*) or obscuring of the Creator by His creation.[71]

It is particularly important to notice Radhakrishnan's position that "the world is not a deception but the occasion for it." He is convinced that there is nothing inherently deceptive or delusive about the world itself. Yet, in his view, the world is too often the occasion for deception, the source of delusion.

69. ERWT, 146. Cf. BG, 217.
70. ERWT, 48.
71. BG, 41.

In the third place, Radhakrishnan interprets *māyā*[5] as a distortion of vision. His meaning becomes clearer when considered in the context of a common, desert experience. Sometimes "puddles" or even "lakes" appear on the road ahead during the summertime. They are especially dangerous at night for passing another car on a two-lane road because they distort distances. During the day they sometimes loom so large that it seems reasonable to stop the car for fear of another desert phenomenon—the flashflood. In a word, the mirages can be dangerous and can affect human action if the truth about them is not known. The mirage is a distortion of vision. So, too, is *māyā*[5], in Radhakrishnan's view. Just as a desert "puddle" can be dangerous if the truth about it is not known, so also Radhakrishnan thinks *māyā*[5] can be dangerous if the truth about it is not known. Whether the "puddles" and *māyā*[5] exist or not is an interesting but infelicitous question. It is interesting because it raises the question "What do we mean when we say something exists?" But it is infelicitous because it is an ontological question in a soteriological context. To borrow a metaphor from medicine, it is like asking a person who is in the hospital dying from cancer: "Does cancer exist?"

Fourthly, Radhakrishnan's interpretation of *māyā*[5] as a distortion of vision is axiological. For him, a distortion of vision is also a distortion of values:

> When the Hindu thinkers ask us to free ourselves from *māyā*, they are asking us to shake off our bondage to the unreal values which are dominating us. They do not ask us to treat life as an illusion or be indifferent to the world's welfare.[72]

Three points are noteworthy here. First, Radhakrishnan does not recommend indifference to the welfare of the world. Instead, he calls on Indians and others to rise up and break the spell of an old tradition—the religious tradition that says a strenuous, active life is opposed to spiritual perfection. Second, he does not think life should be treated as an illusion, a theme which recurs throughout his writings. Third, he thinks that people are dominated by

72. ERWT, 47. Cf. "The doctrine of *māyā* tells us that we fall away from our authentic being if we are lost in the world of empirical objects and earthly desires, turning our back on reality which gives them value." (WUS, 29)

unreal values when they are under the influence of *māyā*^{5}. These last two points appear in a statement which also contains evidence that Radhakrishnan would agree with the comparison of *māyā*^{5} (as a distortion of vision) to a desert "puddle":

> When the illusion of the mirage is dissipated by scientific knowledge, the illusory appearance remains, though it no longer deceives us. We see the same appearance, but give a different value to it. When the illusoriness of the illusion is perceived, it ceases to be an illusion. Whether the forms dissolve themselves in the formless or show themselves to be mere appearances of Brahman, on either view the world is not a mere illusion.[73]

Radhakrishnan's statement that *we see the same appearance*, but *give a different value to it* is evidence for the axiological meaning of *māyā*^{5}. His statement that *the world is not a mere illusion* is further evidence for the thesis of this book.[74]

Finally, Radhakrishnan interprets *māyā*^{5} as ignorance (*avidyā*), specifying that "The concept of māyā is intimately related with that of avidyā."[75] He asserts that the *Śvetāśvatara Upaniṣad* contains the concept designated in this study as *māyā*^{5}: "Māyā in the sense of avidyā is recognised, since the display of the world hides the one spirit in it all."[76] Elsewhere he states quite directly that "When the multiplicity shuts us away from the reality of God,

73. IP, II. 639.

74. Radhakrishnan's writings contain much more evidence for the thesis of this book. Cf. "We see now how the popular conception of the world as *Maya* or illusion is erroneous." (RRCP, 445) Cf. also "The two familiar criticisms that for Hindu thought the world is an illusion (*māyā*), that it is divine (pantheism) cancel each other." (WUS, 27-28) Cf. also "The world is real and not illusory; it is called māyā on account of its nature, since it attracts men to itself and away from God. The servant of God becomes, through the power of māyā, the slave of the world." (IP, II, 763) Cf. also "For the Hindu thinkers, the objective world exists. It is not an illusion. It is real not in being ultimate, but in being a form, an expression of the ultimate. To regard the world as ultimately real is delusion (*moha*)." (ERWT, 31)

75. IP, II, 574. Radhakrishnan points out: "While Śaṁkara uses avidyā and māyā indiscriminately, later Advaitins draw a distinction between the two." (IP, II, 589) Radhakrishnan discusses *māyā* as ignorance throughout his writings. See RRCP, 206, 277; IP, I, 699; IP, II, 572, 582, 610-611; PU, 80-81; BS, 127, 211.

76. IP, I, 513.

māyā is called *avidyā*."[77] The following statement contains further evidence that Radhakrishnan interprets *māyā*[5] both as a source of delusion and as ignorance:

> The world has the tendency to delude us into thinking that it is all, that it is self-dependent, and this delusive character of the world is also designated māyā in the sense of *avidyā*. When we are asked to overcome māyā, it is an injunction to avoid worldliness. Let us not put our trust in the things of this world. Māyā is concerned not with the existence of the world but with its meaning, not with the factuality of the world but with the way in which we look upon it. [78]

Clearly, Radhakrishnan does not interpret *māyā*[5] as an ontological concept. He states that *māyā*[5] is concerned with the world's meaning, not its being. To put it positively, the concept of *māyā*[5] is soteriological and axiological.

Radhakrishnan states that *māyā*[5] is to the cosmos as *avidyā* is to the individual: "While *māyā* covers the whole cosmic manifestation *avidyā* relates to the ignorance of the individual."[79] Radhakrishnan also states that *māyā*[5] is to the objective as *avidyā* is to the subjective:

> When we look at the problem from the objective side, we speak of māyā, and when from the subjective side, we speak of avidyā. Even as Brahman and Ātman are one, so are māyā and avidyā one. The tendency of the human mind to see what is really one as if it were many, is avidyā; but this is common to all individuals.[80]

In short, what Radhakrishnan identifies as a tendency to see the one as the many is what this study designates *māyā*[5] and what Radhakrishnan calls ignorance (*avidyā*).

He uses the metaphor of a chain—a fetter—to express *māyā*[5] as ignorance, cautioning that "*Avidyā* or ignorance of the real

77. BS, 91. Cf. "the individual is bound down by māyā in the sense of *avidyā* or ignorance." (PU, 87)

78. PU, 89. Cf. "When we transcend māyā, time, space and cause do not fall away from us. The world does not disappear, but it only changes its meaning." (IP, I, 548)

79. HPEW, I, 280.

80. IP, II, 587. Cf. "While māyā is more cosmic in significance, *avidyā* is more subjective." (PU, 89)

nature of the world and man's place in it chains us in the bonds of *māyā*."[81] Elsewhere he warns that "If...we make absolutely real what is only relatively real, and mistake a stage for the goal or the final resting-place, we are bound in the chains of *māyā*"[82] and that "No intellectual sophistry can liberate us from the fetters of māyā."[83] The ignorance which concerns Radhakrishnan is the lack of spiritual wisdom and not the lack of intellectual sophistry.

To summarize this section on *māyā*⁵, Radhakrishnan's faith (1) includes the conviction that the phenomena of nature and the drama of history conceal "something more." In his view, the word *māyā* signifies this "veiling" or "cloaking" or "concealing." A soteriological concept, it is identified in this study as *māyā*^{5}. Radhakrishnan thinks *māyā*^{5} is the source of delusion—persistent and false belief about one's self. He repeatedly denies that the world is an ontological illusion—an abnormal or distorted perception. Radhakrishnan characterizes *māyā*^{5} as hiding reality from vision. He portrays it as the source of an alleged delusion of individuality. Referring to Plato's cave parable, Radhakrishnan depicts *māyā*^{5} as a distortion of vision. The distortion is like the optical illusion of a "puddle" in the desert. Perhaps most importantly, *māyā*^{5} as concealment is a soteriological, axiological issue and *not* an ontological one. *Māyā*^{5} is the chain of ignorance (*avidyā*) which fetters humankind from a vision of "something more."

VI. Māyā^6 as One-sided Dependence

Radhakrishnan uses the word *māyā* to signify the one-sided dependence of the world on the Absolute:

> While the world is dependent on Brahman, the latter is not dependent on the world. This one-sided dependence and the logical inconceivability of the relation between the Ultimate Reality and the world are brought out by the word '*māyā*.' [84]

81. PRT, 66.
82. RRCP, 445. Cf. "We require a removal of Avidya or ignorance, a breaking of the bonds of Maya." (PRT, 11)
83. IC, 15. Cf. IP, II, 758.
BG, 38.

Both *māyā*[6] as one-sided dependence and *māyā*[1] as inexplicable mystery are illustrated in this passage. Radhakrishnan declares that Śaṁkara's intention with his rope and snake example was to illustrate this one-sided dependence.[85] Radhakrishnan concludes that Vedantins after Śaṁkara used the term *vivarta* (appearance) to indicate this one-sided relationship.[86] The one-sided dependence of the world on the Absolute, the intention of the rope and snake example, and the difference between *vivarta* and *pariṇāma* (transformation) are explained by Radhakrishnan as follows:

> We have pariṇāma or transformation, when the milk is changed into curds, and vivarta or appearance, when the rope appears as the snake. The different illustrations used by Śaṁkara of the rope and the snake, the shell and the silver, the desert and the mirage, are intended to indicate this one-sided dependence of the effect on the cause and the maintenance of the integrity of the cause. In the case of transformation, the cause and the effect belong to the same order of reality, while in that of appearance the effect is of a different order of being from the cause. The world resides in Brahman even as the illusion of a snake is said to reside in the rope.[87]

It is important to notice Radhakrishnan's position that Śaṁkara's illustrations have a double intention. This study calls attention to Radhakrishnan's view of the double intention of the rope and snake example by dividing the concept of *Māyā*[6] into two parts. *Māyā*[6a] indicates *the one-sided dependence of the effect (the world) on the cause (Brahman)*. *Māyā*[6b] indicates *the maintenance of the integrity of the cause*. This section describes these two aspects of *Māyā*[6] separately.

First of all, *Māyā*[6a] indicates Radhakrishnan's view regarding the one-sided dependence of the world on the Absolute. Convinced about the reality of an unseen world, Radhakrishnan argues that behind the phenomena of nature and the drama of

85. IP, II, 570; ERWT, 91; HPEW, I, 278; Schilpp, ed., 800; BS, 33, 141. S. O. Ramakrishnan agrees: "To illustrate this one-sided dependence of the effect upon the cause, Sankara gives various examples like the rope-snake, shell-silver, etc." (*The Vedānta Kesari* 49 [June 1962]: 108).

86. HPEW, I, 278. Cf. appendix V, section one, paragraph two.

87. IP, II, 570.

history is this "something more" on which the phenonena are based. He judges that the discursive intellect cannot grasp in its entirety the content of this phrase "something more." But in so far as ultimate reality can be caught in the net of words, he refers to it as changelessness which paradoxically grows and bursts forth, unity and continuity, consciousness, the whole, harmony, and truth. His interpretation of *māyā*[6a] is that the changing world depends on the changeless, the world of multiplicity depends on the unity behind it, the material world (*prakṛti*) depends on consciousness (*puruṣa*), the parts depend on the whole, behind all discord is harmony, and behind the veil of untruth is truth. Radhakrishnan proposes that ultimate reality be conceived as having four poises—*Brahman*, *Īśvara*, *Hiraṇyagarbha*, and *Virāṭ*. He proposes further that *Virāṭ* depends on Brahman since "To look upon the world as self-sufficient is to be caught in *māyā*."[88] Guarding against the hermeneutics of illusion, he narrates: "The Upaniṣads support the doctrine of māyā only in the sense that there is an underlying reality containing all elements from the personal God to the telegraph post."[89] *Māyā*[6a] is illustrated graphically in the philosophy professor's proposition that "The Absolute alone has non-created divine reality; all else is dependent, created reality. This is the significance of the doctrine of māyā."[90] Another passage illustrates not only Radhakrishnan's *māyā*[6a] hermeneutics but also his view that the world is not an illusion:

> We see, there is a great difference between this view, which ascribes reality,—though a dependent reality,—to the finite world, and the Maya view, which reduces it to an illusion. The world which our intellect reveals to us is real, though its reality is limited and partial. The finite world is not absolutely real, for it demands something else on which it depends.[91]

With a modernist's loyalty to tradition, Radhakrishnan argues against the view of Maya held by Prabhu Dutt Shastri and others that the sole reality of Brahman reduces the world to an illusion.

Before leaving Radhakrishnan's interpretation of *māyā*[6a],

88. BS, 137.
89. IP, I, 197.
90. Schilpp, ed., p. 41.
91. "The VP and the DM," p. 441.

it is important to notice that references in his writings to *māyā* as phenomenality are illustrations of what this study calls *māyā*[6a]. Incidentally, when a modern philosopher uses the word *phenomenon*, he or she probably has in mind Kant's distinction between the *phenomenal* and *noumenal*. Radhakrishnan's reference to "the wellknown doctrine of the phenomenality of the world (*māyā*)"[92] probably draws on Kant's distinction. Radhakrishnan states that "The abstract expression of this phenomenality of the world is māyā,"[93] further exemplifying *māyā*[6a]. Sir Sarvepalli's reference to the fragility of the universe illustrates *māyā*[6a] as well as his position that the world is not an illusion:

> The phenomenal character of the empirical self and the world answering to it is denoted by the word *māyā*, which signifies the fragility of the universe. *Māyā* does not mean that the empirical world with the selves in it is an illusion, for the whole effort of the cosmos is directed to and sustained by the one supreme self, which though distinct from everything is implicated in everything.[94]

In keeping with the overall thesis of this book, Radhakrishnan rejects the interpretation of *māyā* which says that the empirical world with the selves in it is an illusion.

Sir Sarvepalli's references to the mutability and the passingness of all things are also illustrations of *māyā*[6a]. For instance he remarks that "The mutability of things which is part of the connotation of the word *māyā* is a well-known theme in the world's literature"[95] and that "Every object is tending to pass away from itself to something else....This character of the world is enough to indicate its nature as appearance, or māyā."[96] The mutability and passingness of all things is also expressed in Radhakrishnan's statement: "When we speak of the world as *māyā* we refer to the feeling of the vanity of life."[97] The following statement

92. ERWT, 223.
93. IP, II, 564.
94. WUS, 25.
95. ERWT, 85.
96. IP, II, 532. Cf. "In other words, the things of the world are not eternal. The world is *māyā* , i.e., passes away, but God is eternal." (ERWT, 86)
97. BS, 136.

further supports the thesis that Radhakrishnan's *māyā* hermeneutics includes *māyā*[6a] as the one-sided dependence of the world on Brahman; it also supports the overall thesis of this book that Radhakrishnan thinks the world is not an illusion:

> The doctrine of māyā declares that the world is dependent on and derived from the ultimate reality. It has the character of perpetual passing away, while the real is exempt from change. It has therefore a lower status than the supreme itself. In no case is its existence to be confused with illusory being or non-existence. Even Śaṁkara [*sic*], who advocates the theory of māyā, carefully distinguishes the phenomenal existence of the world from the being of Brahman and the non-being of dreams, illusions, etc. Besides, many other interpreters of the Vedānta repudiate the doctrine of māyā even in this limited sense.[98]

The clause *in no case is its (the world's) existence to be confused with illusory being or non-existence* is another variation on the theme which Radhakrishnan repeats again and again throughout all his writings.

This study has already noted Radhakrishnan's cosmogonic theory of emanation in which the one becomes many without being affected by the many. This is the meaning of the concept designated *māyā*[6b]. It signifies the maintenance of the integrity of the cause. For instance, the translator of the Upaniṣads pens:

> Māyā in this view states the fact that *Brahman* without losing his integrity is the basis of the world. Though devoid of all specifications, *Brahman* is the root cause of the universe. 'If a thing cannot subsist apart from something else, the latter is the essence of that thing.' The cause is logically prior to the effect. Questions of temporal beginning and growth are subordinate to this relation of ground and consequent. The world does not carry its own meaning. To regard it as final and ultimate is an act of ignorance.[99]

98. Ferm, ed., *Religion in Transition*, pp. 22-23.

99. PU, 80. Cf. PU, 566. Cf. also "If Brahman is to be viewed as the cause of the world it is only in the sense that the world cannot be explained apart from Brahman, though the latter is in no way touched by the world of appearance." (*Encyclopedia Britannica*, 14th ed., s.v. "Indian Philosophy," by S. Radhakrishnan).

Clearly, Radhakrishnan considers Brahman to be the root cause of the universe. He conceives Brahman's causal activity as having no effect on the cause. Radhakrishnan's sixfold summary of *māyā* in his "Introduction" to The *Bhagavadgītā* (appendix III), the paradigm for the six meanings of *māyā* described in this chapter, begins: "If the Supreme Reality is unaffected by the events of the world,..." This lack of affect in the relation of the world to Brahman is the meaning of *māyā*^{6b}. Radhakrishnan's cosmogonic theory of emanation in which the integrity of the cause is maintained may be clarified by considering his concept of reality in four poises. Radhakrishnan theorizes that Brahman as causal activity is Īśvara. He thinks that Īśvara's power of self-becoming gives rise to the world-spirit (*Hiraṇyagarbha*) and the world (*Virāṭ*). *Māyā*^{6b} means that while Brahman has an effect on *Virāṭ*, *Virāṭ* has no effect on Brahman.

To summarize this section on *māyā*^{6} as one-sided dependence, Radhakrishnan thinks that the world depends on the Absolute and that the Absolute does not depend on the world. He argues that this one-sided dependence is what Śaṁkara means by his example of the rope and the snake. The concept *māyā*^{6a} indicates Radhakrishnan's view that behind the phenomena of nature and the drama of history there is "something more" on which the phenomena are based. References in Radhakrishnan's writings to *phenomenality* as the meaning of *māyā* illustrate *māyā*^{6a}. His references to the *mutability* and the *passingness of all things* also illustrate *māyā*^{6a}. *Māyā*^{6b} indicates Radhakrishnan's view that the integrity of the cause is always maintained. According to his theory of emanation, Virāṭ as the effect does not affect Brahman as the cause.

In summary, the writings of Sarvepalli Radhakrishnan contain at least six meanings of the term *māyā*. This study has introduced six superscripts in order to distinguish the meanings. The model used in this book originates with Sir Sarvepalli's own sixfold summary of the meanings of *māyā* in his "Introduction" to his translation of *The Bhagavadgītā* (appendix III).

Māyā^{1} means inexplicable mystery. It is an epistemological concept which indicates Radhakrishnan's position that the relation between the world and the Absolute cannot be explained. Regarding ultimate cosmogonic questions, Radhakrishnan recommends that an attitude of wise agnosticism be adopted. He generalizes that people are bound Prometheus-like to the rock of mystery by the chains of their finite minds.

Nevertheless, Radhakrishnan cannot resist the temptation to offer a theoretical explanation for the origin of the world. *Māyā*^{2} is a cosmogonic concept which means the power of self-becoming (*ātmavibhūti*). *Māyā*^{2} also means the power of self-expression, the power of self-manifestation, the power of creation (*sṛṣti*), and creative energy (*śakti*). In Radhakrishnan's view, the power of self-becoming is inherent in Īśvara.

Māyā^3 signifies the duality of consciousness (*puruṣa*) and matter (*prakṛti*) which Radhakrishnan posits as a characteristic of all things. It is a "uniting" concept in that he uses it to unite the Sāṁkhya and Vedānta *darśanas*. In order to visualize *māyā*^{3} this study suggests that Radhakrishnan views all things as if they were on the curve of an ellipse whose two foci are consciousness and matter.

Māyā^4 means primal matter, a phrase which Radhakrishnan equates with *lower prakṛti*. He tries to unite Sāṁkhya dualism and his own non-dualism by suggesting that an alleged Absolute breaks up its own wholeness into self and not-self, Puruṣa and *prakṛti*, Īśvara and *māyā*^{1} respectively.

Māyā^5 means concealment. It is an axiological and soteriological concept, not an ontological one. Radhakrishnan is convinced that phenomena hide, veil, cloak, and conceal "something more" on which the phenomena are based. He presents *māyā*^{5} as the source of an alleged delusion of individuality and describes it as a distortion of vision. It is like the illusion of a "puddle" in the desert. Radhakrishnan interprets *māyā*^{5} as ignorance (*avidyā*) and warns his readers about its capacity to chain and fetter. *Māyā*^{5} is to the cosmos as *avidyā* is to the individual.

This study splits the meaning of *māyā*^{6} into two parts. *Māyā*^{6a} means the one-sided dependence of the effect on the cause. *Māyā*^{6b} means the maintenance of the integrity of the cause. Radhakrishnan thinks that the world—symbolized by Virāṭ—depends on the Absolute and that the Absolute—symbolized by Brahman—does not depend on the world. Radhakrishnan explains that this one-sided dependence is the meaning of Śaṁkara's snake and rope illustration.

5

Radhakrishnan's Achievement in Perspective

This chapter evaluates Sarvepalli Radhakrishnan's *māyā* hermeneutics. The six meanings of *māyā* are evaluated separately in sections one through six, respectively. Section seven gives a general estimate of Radhakrishnan's doctrine of *māyā* as well as the strengths and weaknesses of his overall philosophical position.

I. Māyā^1 : An Epistemological Issue

Māyā^1 as inexplicable mystery is basically an epistemological concept, inviting attention to the question: "How do we know what we know ?" Chapter one described Radhakrishnan's faith (1)—his attitude of conviction—regarding the reality of an unseen world behind the flux of phenomena. Many variations on this theme have been noted such as Radhakrishnan's confession that behind the phenomena of nature and the drama of history is an unseen spiritual power. Therefore, the basic issue in this evaluation of Radhakrishnan's *māyā*^{1} concept is : "How do we know anything about the alleged reality of an unseen world behind the phenomenal flux ?" In other words: "How do we get our minds around the idea of an alleged 'something more' ?"

Radhakrishnan supposes that religious knowledge is intuitive, equating intuitive knowledge and integral insight. He takes the position that integral insight is gained in a mode of presentational immediacy, implying that reality in its entirety cannot be grasped mediately through discursive intellect. On the journey toward the realm of religious knowledge and certitude, suggests Radhakrishnan, one passes through the land of discursive intellect in order to gain certain knowledge in the land of intuition. He contends that one is able to "see things from the Supreme Identity that lies behind the terrestrial process."[1] This contention is the major weakness in Radhakrishnan's epistemology, for how can things be seen from the Supreme Identity? In short, how can we see things as though we were God? Radhakrishnan's faith (3)—*aham brahmāsmi* (I am divine) and *tat tvam asi* (That art thou)—allows him to argue from the divine point of view. On the other hand, Christian faith includes the attitude of great conviction that God and persons are separate realities. The Biblical doctrine of creation implies that God and persons are not identical. Therefore, responsible Christians refrain from makking assertions as if it were possible to see things from God's point of view. Religious knowledge claims are based on information garnered from human experience, but who knows with certainty anything about God's experience? Incidentally, fairness to Radhakrishnan requires his opponents to notice his temperate attitude of wise agnosticism reflected in the phrase from *Ṛg Veda* X. 129—*ko veda*? (Who knows?)

Radhakrishnan's epistemology includes the view that reality and truth are many-sided. He shares with the Jains an *anekāntavādist* point of view. Furthermore, Radhakrishnan often takes the position that reality and truth are of just two kinds—penultimate and ultimate. Bifurcating reality into two ontological levels, he uses nine adjectives to describe that which is penultimate—conditioned, contingent, created, dependent, empirical, finite, manifested, phenomenal, and relative. There are many illustrations of Radhakrishnan's split-level way of thinking, but two will suffice. He explains that "Reality, according to the Vedanta, has two aspects, the higher and the lower, the fixed and the chang-

1. This statement appears in chapter four, section I. All undocumented statements by Radhakrishnan appearing in this chapter are taken from the respective sections in chapter four which deal with the meaning of *māyā* under discussion.

ing, the absolute and the relative."[2] Secondly, he observes that "In man there is a struggle between the higher and the lower... He is an amphibious animal living in two worlds."[3] The radical difference between Radhakrishnan and his opponents lies in the fact that Radhakrishnan makes knowledge claims based on trans-human experience. He "tells it like it is" from the ultimate, absolute, divine point of view, from an alleged Supreme Identity that lies behind the terrestrial process. Radhakrishnan claims to speak with the authority of one who knows what God knows. The Christian whose faith is tempered by reason shudders with horror at the prospect of conversing with someone who claims to know exactly what God knows. Radhakrishnan's rejoinder would be that there really is no basic difference between Hinduism and Christianity. He would argue that *Brahman* and *God* are simply two different symbols pointing to the same ultimate reality—a reality which is identical with the true self. After all, claims Radhakrishnan with his mentor Tagore, there is an ultimate unity among all religions. But his epistemological basis for making this claim is that he can see this alleged unity from his "ultimate" point of view. Hindus and Christians cease to communicate when the dialogue reaches this point. This basic criticism of Radhakrishnan's epistemology—that it fails because it rests on a split-level view of ontological reality—will have served a useful purpose if it underscores the radical difference between Hinduism and Christianity on this issue. There is no justification for students of the world's faiths and cumulative traditions to argue in favor of their own particular tradition by claiming access to a body of knowledge which is available only to believers in their own particular tradition. We would do well to remember two points made by W. C. Smith. He suggests that "no statement about a religion is valid unless it can be acknowledged by that religion's believers."[4] However, he warns that "The reverse is certainly not true."[5]

2. "The Ethics of the Bhagavadgītā and Kant," *International Journal of Ethics* 21 (July 1911): 466.

3. RRCP, 431.

4. Wilfred Cantwell Smith, "Comparative Religion: Whither—and Why?" in *The History of Religions: Essays in Methodology*, eds., Mircea Eliade and Joseph M. Kitagawa (Chicago: University of Chicago, 1959; also published as a Phoenix Book), p. 42.

5. Ibid., p. 43.

Radhakrishnan's epistemological concept of *māyā*[1] as inexplicable mystery can now be evaluated more specifically. He contends that the relationship between Brahman and the world, between poise one and poise four of what he calls Supreme Reality, cannot be explained : "We can never understand how the ultimate reality is related to the world of plurality, since the two are heterogeneous, and every attempt at explanation is bound to fail." Here is another illustration of Radhakrishnan's split-level ontology. He goes even further. As if our inability to explicate the relationship between deity and the world were not enough, Radhakrishnan asserts that we are unable to explicate *any* relation between *any* two. He argues in this vein when he is being strictly metaphysical. Radhakrishnan's *advaita vedānta* monism prevents him from acknowledging the absolute reality of any relation whatsoever since this acknowledgement would require a logically necessary acknowledgement of the absolute reality of two relata. This study has noted Radhakrishnan's statement to the effect that every moment of his or her life the Hindu is required to remember the ultimate oneness of things. In a word, this is Hindu faith (1). To put this in more philosophical terms, Radhakrishnan is thoroughly convinced that the real is the one. But many philosophers in both the West and the East are equally convinced that the real is the many. Therefore, the pluralist philosopher rejects Radhakrishnan's assertion regarding the inexplicability of *any* relation between *any* two. While the relationship between deity and the world is admittedly very difficult to explain, the difficulty is not caused by the alleged inexplicability of *any* relation between *any* two. Not surprisingly, much of Radhakrishnan's early criticism of Western philosophers, especially in *The Reign of Religion in Contemporary Philosophy*, revolves around this difference between his own monism and their dualism or pluralism.

To this point, Radhakrishnan's achievement has received several negative comments. However, his achievement also deserves a highly significant positive comment. As a Hindu modernist Radhakrishnan rejects the interpretation of *māyā* which says that the world is an illusion. Chapter four reported Radhakrishnan's statement: "It is one thing to say that the secret of existence... is a mystery, and another to dismiss the whole changing universe as a mere mirage." He deserves a particularly positive valuation for distinguishing between *mystery* and *mirage*. The epistemological proposition that the God-world relationship is an inexplicable mystery does not require or imply the proposition that the world is a mere mirage—an illusion. *Illusion* is used here to signify *a distorted or abnormal perception.* Radhakrishnan contends, and rightly so, that the world is neither a distorted nor an abnormal perception even though the world is rife with myriad mysteries—wonderful, awesome, inexplicable processes. Radhakrishnan argues that Śaṁkara's snake and rope illustration points to the one-sided dependence of the world on Brahman and that it should not be used to illustrate an alleged illusoriness of the world.

II. Māyā[2] : A Cosmogonic Issue

Power of self-becoming is Radhakrishnan's translation of *ātmavibhūti. Ātmavibhūti* means "the arising, developing, manifesting, expanding, or appearing of the self." Into focus comes a cosmogonic picture of Ātman arising or expanding and becoming the scheme of things entire. It has been noted that Radhakrishnan's ontology contains an interesting question: "Is reality changeless or growing?" If Ātman possesses the inherent power to arise or expand and thus to become the universe, the identity of Ātman and Brahman would require that Brahman, too, have this inherent power of change. In fact, Radhakrishnan derives Brahman from the root *bṛh* which means "to grow, to burst forth." Therefore, a positive valuation can be assigned to all those cosmogonic passages in which Radhakrishnan is consistent in describing the reality of Ātman and Brahman as a changing reality. Unfortunately, he often takes the more traditional *advaita vedānta* position that the Absolute is changeless.

Between Radhakrishnan and most Christian theologians lies the cosmogonic issue of emanation versus creation. Radhakrishnan points out that the Sanskrit word *sṛṣṭi* means *emanation, letting loose*. Yet *sṛṣṭi* most often gets translated *creation*, a loose translation resulting in confusion. An alleged self (Ātman) from which the world is let loose gets confused with a God who struggles to create. It might be argued that the Christian doctrine of creation out of nothing (*creatio ex nihilo*) is not unlike

Radhakrishnan's doctrine of *māyā*²—the doctrine of Īśvara's power to mold forms out of the formless. However, this comparison produces additional confusion. Brahman and God are not identical concepts. Neither are Īśvara and God identical. While it is true that *māyā*²—the power of "creation" (*sṛṣṭi*)—is cosmogonic agency which inheres in Īśvara, it is also true that Īśvara is powerless apart from Brahman. In fact, Radhakrishnan contends that the ontological reality of Īśvara (poise two) is inconceivable apart from the ontological reality of Brahman (poise one). To the contrary, neither God's power to create nor God's ontological reality is conceivable as a dependent part of another power or another ontological reality. In short, Radhakrishnan's theory of emanation and the Biblical and Quranic theories of creation differ with respect to the dependence or independence of deity. Īśvara's power to make or mold forms out of the formless depends on Brahman whereas God's power to create is independent.

*Māyā*² functions in Radhakrishnan's system as the principle of what this study will call *upagainstness*. Radhakrishnan uses other, more familiar words to interpret *māyā*², describing it as the power of self-expression, the self-sundering of the Eternal, the self-limiting power of the Absolute, the self-distinction residing in the very heart of reality, the dividing force, and the finitising principle. In order to explore the way in which *māyā*² functions, the reader is invited to recall some of the background concepts in Radhakrishnan's ontology. He posits the ontological reality of unity, consciousness, harmony, and the whole. The philosophical problem is to explain how unity lets loose disunity, how consciousness generates the non-conscious, how harmony turns into cacophany, and how the whole breaks into parts. *Māyā*² is Radhakrishnan's solution. It is the principle of upagainstness used by primal consciousness to let loose individual consciousnesses. In other words, primal consciousness comes up against itself in the process of the emanation of the universe. Radhakrishnan requires a principle of limitation to explain how the primal one limits itself as it becomes the many. *Māyā*² is this principle of limitation. It is the power, *śakti*, or energy—inherent in Īśvara—which emanates the "other" from the self (Ātman). The function of *māyā*² is to limit the Absolute, to sunder the Eternal, to divide "that one," and to make finite what is infinite. In short, the Absolute comes up against *māyā*² as it emanates or lets loose the universe.

Unfortunately, Radhakrishnan's achievement in this respect must be given a negative valuation. His monism prevents him from granting absolute ontological status to the power of self-becoming—*māyā*². Since this study rejects his split-level way of thinking which bifurcates reality into two ontological levels, it cannot grant an ontological status to *māyā*² which would put it on an allegedly lower level of reality. What, then, is *māyā*² which Radhakrishnan conceives as the power of self-becoming? This study concludes that it is a stop-gap measure taken by *advaita vedāntins* to provide an explanation for the fact of the many in light of the *advaita vedānta* contention regarding the sole reality of the one.

Until now this section has focused on the function of *māyā*² in the cosmogonic process. However, Radhakrishnan's attitude toward the result of the cosmogonic process is equally significant. It deserves a decidedly positive valuation. He draws a distinction between a *likeness* on the one hand and an *illusion* or a *mirage* on the other. *Śvetāśvatara Upaniṣad* IV.10 describes God as *māyin* and Radhakrishnan declares that "Here *māyā* is used in the sense in which the *Ṛg Veda* employs it, the divine art or power by which the divinity makes a likeness of the eternal prototypes or ideas inherent in his nature." In short, God's power of *māyā*² is the power to make likenesses of ideas which are already inherent in God. For Radhakrishnan, these likenesses comprise the world. But the likenesses are not illusions or mirages. The cumulative tradition of the Hindus contains many references to Brahman's sport (*līlā*) in the cosmogonic process. Rabindranath Tagore is particularly fond of referring to God as a creative artist. The creative activity of Īśvara can be compared with sculpting. In a moment of inspiration the sculptor conceives. He or she then continues to struggle—sometimes for years—in order to shape the clay, wood, bronze, or marble into a likeness of the original conception. The application of technique which follows the moment of inspiration is a necessary part of the creative struggle, and good artists are willing to continue embracing the technical struggle. In this analogy, the sculptor is Īśvara and the piece of sculpture is the world. It is a *likeness*. Radhakrishnan rejects the illusional interpretation of *māyā* because he does not believe that Īśvara as artist makes illusory likenesses any more than a sculptor makes likenesses which are merely distorted or abnormal perceptions. To the contrary, Radhakrishnan affirms the likenesses with a fervor which is reminiscent of Tagore's romantic attachment to the natural world. In *The Philosophy of Rabindranath Tagore*, Radhakrishnan displays unbridled enthusiasm for Tagore's world-affirming stance. The reader is invited to recall the strong influence of Tagore's vision of ethics on the young Radhakrishnan's interpretation of *māyā*.

III. Māyā³ : Sāṁkhya Dualism and Vedānta Non-Dualism

Māyā³ as duality of consciousness (*puruṣa*) and matter (*prakṛti*) is the least important meaning of *māyā* in Radhakrishnan's hermeneutics. However, it raises an important issue. This study argues that Radhakrishnan uses *māyā³* in his attempt to unite the Sāṁkhya and Vedānta *darśanas*. The issue raised by Radhakrishnan's concept of *māyā³* is whether Sāṁkhya dualism and Vedānta non-dualism ever can be united. The larger issue raised by Radhakrishnan's use of *māyā³* as a "uniting" concept is whether unity—as Radhakrishnan supposes—is ontologically the nature of the case. Chapter one noted that the problem of *māyā* is primarily an axiological and soteriological problem. However, this evaluation of Radhakrishnan's interpretation of *māyā* would be incomplete if it were to bypass the ontological issue altogether.

Radhakrishnan's concept of reality in four poises—Brahman, Īśvara, Hiraṇyagarbha, and Virāṭ—is of paramount importance for his systematic theology. Research for this book supports the conclusion that it is Radhakrishnan's most important contribution to the field of Indian ontology. For instance, it helps clarify his meaning when he explains that "All things partake of the duality of being and nonbeing from Puruṣottama downwards." The phrase *duality of being and nonbeing* parallels the phrase *duality of consciousness and matter*. The phrase *from Puruṣottama downwards* can be understood as a reference to Īśvara, Hiraṇyagarbha, and Virāṭ. Radhakrishnan contends that all things from Īśvara downwards display *māyā*[3] as duality of being and non-being. Brahman alone—poise one—is non-dual.

Radhakrishnan's references to consciousness as *puruṣa* and matter as *prakṛti* indicate that his concept of *māyā*[3] is shaped by Sāṁkhya thought. He writes: "Since the Lord is able to produce the universe by means of the two elements of his being, prakṛti and puruṣa, matter and consciousness, they are said to be māyā (higher and lower) [*sic*] of God." The Sāṁkhya theory of evolution rests on a dualism of *puruṣa* and *prakṛti*, and Radhakrishnan's formulation of *māyā*[3] is an attempt to incorporate the Sāṁkhya categories into his own Vedānta non-dualism (*advaita vedānta*). The phrase *higher and lower* as a modifier of *māyā* does not appear elsewhere in Radhakrishnan's writings. Therefore, its meaning is rather unclear. However, it is clear that Radhakrishnan subordinates Sāṁkhya dualism to Vedānta non-dualism. He contends that *the Lord is able to produce the universe by means of the two elements of His being*. Radhakrishnan envisions a deity which includes both consciousness and matter. Again, his concept of reality in four poises helps to clarify his meaning. Īśvara (poise two) can be understood as *the Lord* whose power of self-becoming (*māyā*[2]) enables him or her to produce the universe. The two elements of Īśvara's being are consciousness and matter. Consciousness can be understood as poise three (Hiraṇyagarbha) and matter can be understood as poise four (Virāṭ). If these three parallels are granted, then Radhakrishnan—using his concept of reality in four poises—has incorporated successfully Sāṁkhya dualism into Vedānta non-dualism.

However, Radhakrishnan's achievement in this area must be given a negative valuation. Sāṁkhya dualism and Vedānta non-dualism cannot be united because Sāṁkhya thought gives absolute ontological status to both consciousness and matter whereas Radhakrishnan gives absolute ontological status to consciousness only. Reality (whether changeless or growing), unity and continuity, consciousness, the whole, harmony, and truth are the basic background concepts in Radhakrishnan's ontology. Matter is conspicuous by its absence. Even though Radhakrishnan's interpretation of *māyā* discards the idea that the material world is an illusion, it does not categorize matter as being ultimately real. In Radhakrishnan's thought, matter is neither unreal nor real. It is penultimately real. Nine adjectives used by Radhakrishnan to distinguish the penultimate from the ultimate have been noted. At one point or another, Radhakrishnan uses all nine adjectives to modify *matter*. Unless one agrees with Radhakrishnan to bifurcate reality into two ontological levels, it is impossible to unify Sāṁkhya duality and Vedānta non-duality. Using two levels of reality, *advaita vedāntins* are able to affirm the absolute ontological status of consciousness on the upper level and the relative ontological status of matter on the lower level. But Sāṁkhya thought does not place consciousness and matter on two different ontological levels. Sāṁkhya contends that both *puruṣa* and *prakṛti* are real in every sense.

IV. Māyā[4] : Matter is Real as Part of the Whole

The lasting value of Radhakrishnan's *māyā* hermeneutics is that it helps to shape a modern Hindu system in which matter is real when seen as part of the whole. The undesirability of Radhakrishnan's interpretation of *māyā* is that it perpetuates a worldview in which matter is considered to be real *only* when it is conceived as part of an alleged whole.

This study notes that the whole is particularly important in Radhakrishnan's writings before 1932. Chapter three, section two contains eight statements which describe the whole as a background concept in Radhakrishnan's ontology, including: "The whole is the explanation of all its parts or stages. It alone is ultimately real while all else has a dependent and derivative reality."[6] For Radhakrishnan, the *whole* is not matter. There is no way in which he can be construed as a materialist. Therefore, Radhakrishnan's position is that matter has dependent and derivative reality. While matter is not independently real, neither is it illusory.

This interpretation of *māyā*[4] as primal matter deserves a positive valuation when compared with Prabhu Dutt Shastri's interpretation of *māyā*. Shastri dismisses as illusory everything but Brahman. Fairness to Shastri requires that the soteriological intention of such dismissals be recognized. Similarly, Nāgārjuna

6. RRCP, 85.

has a soteriological purpose for inviting Buddhist attention away from the *dharma* aggregates with alleged *svabhava* (self-existence) posited by Abhidharma philosophers in order to invite attention towards the emptiness (*śūnyatā*) of all things. However, soteriology cannot be divorced from ontology. The ontological dirt of Shastri's interpretation of Māyā cannot be swept under a carpet. Insistence on the illusoriness of the world has serious consequences. It breeds world-negation, world-denial, and contempt for physical matter. It destroys the impetus for ethical struggle. It may have been the main cause for India's late start at industrialization and technological revolution. After all, Shastri would argue, why expend great amounts of energy to industrialize when industrial products are nothing more than mere illusions?

On the other hand, Radhakrishnan's interpretation of *māyā*[4] as primal matter deserves negative valuation when it is compared with the secular worldview circulating in scientific, educational, social, cultural, and governmental institutions. A basic ingredient of this secular worldview is that matter has independent ontological status. In other words, matter exists with or without Brahman—the whole. Radhakrishnan rejects this view. He contends that matter is real only as part of the whole. Fairness to Radhakrishnan requires that we note the distinction he draws between *existence* and *reality*. He readily acknowledges that matter exists on an allegedly lower ontological level. But he refuses to acknowledge that matter is absolutely, independently real. Heinrich Zimmer gets the credit for pointing out correctly that Indian philosophy has come through no *Götterdammerung*—no twilight of the gods. More specifically, Radhakrishnan's *Weltanschauung* lacks the basic ingredient of a viable, secular worldview—the complete, absolute independence of matter from spirit. Research for this study points to the conclusion that Radhakrishnan's refusal to grant matter an independent ontological status is a refusal which brought him great intellectual distress. In so many ways he is open to a modernist, secular approach to philosophical problems. Yet his own faith and cumulative tradition prevent him from interpreting *māyā* so as to grant the material world absolute reality apart from Brahman. In this respect, his interpretation of *māyā*[4] as primal matter is not a total success. It suffers from undue reverence for the ancient forms of Indian thought which include the idea of *māyā* as primal matter dependent on primal spirit.

Modern philosophy with its view of the independent reality of matter does not necessarily reject the reality of spirit. To the contrary, some modern thinkers recognize an obligation to articulate clearly the relation between spirit and matter—between God and the world. Alfred North Whitehead's monumental *Process and Reality* comes to mind. However, many modern philosophers contend that the articulation of this relation will be completely inane if we do not begin with the assumption that the relata to be related are independently real. Radhakrishnan's non-dualist position is that matter is real only as a part of the whole. He solves the problem of relating God and the world by defining the material world as already related to God. His solution by definition will satisfy those who already share his *advaita vedānta* viewpoint. But considered from an objective, press box point of view, his solution suffers from the arbitrariness inherent in all definitional glosses.

V. Māyā^5 : A Soteriological Issue

An evaluation of *māyā*^{5} raises soteriological questions. Does the world conceal "something more" and thereby prevent liberation or release (*mokṣa*)? Does matter veil spirit and thereby stunt spiritual growth? Does phenomenal existence hide absolute reality and thereby destroy the possibility of relating to or uniting with that which is absolutely real? In short, is the world of objective forms an illusion which distorts perception of deity?

Compared with Prabhu Dutt Shastri's interpretation of *māyā*, Radhakrishnan's *māyā* hermeneutics deserves a positive valuation. Radhakrishnan's achievement is that he separates the issue of the world's ontological status from the issue of the world's axiological status. Science, philosophy, and religion are separate areas of human experience. Therefore, the scientific investigation of the factual should be separated from the philosophical and religious investigations of the meaningful and the valuable. Radhakrishnan's position is that liberation from the grip of worldly values does not require ontological world-denial or ontological world-negation.

On the other hand, Radhakrishnan's interpretation of *māyā* deserves a negative valuation because it is based on the assumption that the reality of the world depends on the reality of God. Radhakrishnan never admits that matter can exist without spirit. His position is that the reality of spirit is certain and that the reality of matter depends on the reality of spirit. To the contrary, his opponents take the position that the reality of matter is certain and that the reality of spirit is also certain. The tough philosophical problem is to construct a coherent system which relates the two.

The reader's attention is now invited to some details in Radhakrishnan's interpretation of *māyā*[5] as concealment. The *locus classicus* of *māyā*[5] in Radhakrishnan's writings is a statement which appears in an exposition of *mokṣa*. Radhakrishnan describes Śaṁkara's view of "release" and from context it can be assumed that he is describing his own view as well:

> Māyā as concealment has no power over the liberated soul. When the certainty of the oneness of Brahman and the Ātman is reached by anubhava, the tie which binds us to forms is cut, and the forms cease to be attractive on their own account. They may remain and will remain, so long as the senses are alive and intellect operates, but there is no need to connect them with the intuited Brahman. When the illusion of the mirage is dissipated by scientific knowledge, the illusory appearance remains, though it no longer deceives us. We see the same appearance, but give a different value to it. When the illusoriness of the illusion is perceived, it ceases to be an illusion. Whether the forms dissolve themselves in the formless or show themselves to be mere appearances of Brahman, on either view the world is not a mere illusion.[7]

Since this statement raises important issues for Radhakrishnan's overall interpretation of *māyā*, it will be discussed in several parts.

Radhakrishnan's position expressed in the first sentence is in keeping with the general Hindu position that even the gods themselves have no power over the perfectly enlightened *rishis*.

7. IP, II, 639.

The second sentence contains two recurring themes in Radhakrishnan's faith: (a) the oneness of Brahman and Ātman: and (b) the certainty which is reached through the experience of anubhava—integral insight. That oneness (unity) has absolute ontological status is the most important ontological concept in Radhakrishnan's entire system of thought. That certainty is reached by anubhava (integral insight) is the most important epistemological concept in his thought.

The second sentence also contains a reference to *forms*. Radhakrishnan reports that forms cease to be attractive after the experience of anubhava. In some respects, the entire issue of *māyā* is contained in this one phrase.Radhakrishnan's positive achievement in interpreting *māyā* is his articulation of the position that when forms cease to be attractive they do not necessarily cease to exist. The fact that they cease to be attractive indicates a change in the soteriological status of those whom they formerly attracted. It does not indicate a change in the ontological status of the forms. This is Radhakrishnan's meaning when he writes: "Māyā is concerned not with the existence of the world but with its meaning, not with the factuality of the world but with the way in which we look upon it."[8] Radhakrishnan's contention that religion is personal transformation has been noted. The fable of the tiger cub comes to mind. Liberation or release (*mokṣa*), explains Radhakrishnan, is personal transformation after which the forms cease to be attractive. After liberation, he observes, the forms no longer conceal Brahman.

In the block quotation above, Radhakrishnan reasons that "When the illusion of the mirage is dissipated by scientific knowledge, the illusory appearance remains, though it no longer deceives us. We see the same appearance, but give a different value to it." A puddle in the desert is a mirage. The mirage is dissipated by scientific knowledge when we learn that the mirage is caused by heat rising from the desert. Yet the mirage does not disappear once we know that the mirage depends on and arises from the desert heat. In this analogy, the mirage is the world and the desert heat is Brahman. Radhakrishnan argues that just as the ontological reality of the mirage depends on and arises from

8. PU, 89.

the desert heat, so also the ontological reality of the world depends on and arises from Brahman. He takes the analogy one step further. Just as the mirage does not disappear when scientific knowledge is gained about that upon which it depends, neither does the world disappear when intuitive knowledge is gained about that upon which it depends. The world remains, but it is valued differently.

Radhakrishnan interprets *māyā*[5] as a source of delusion. This study coins the phrase *delusions of individuality* in order to describe the content of what Radhakrishnan suggests is a persistent and false belief about the human self. He contends that people delude themselves if they think of themselves as individuals. In his view, individual persons are in touch with reality only when they realize that their true identity—their true self—is devoid of individuality. In other words, Radhakrishnan proposes that individuals get in touch with reality when they renounce and deny their existence as individuals. Unfortuantely, his view of the oneness of Ātman (the "true" self) and Brahman informs and controls his view of individuals. While he grants that individuals exist on a lower ontological level, he denies that they exist on a higher ontological level. On the lower level he puts the relatively real and on the upper level he puts the absolutely real. This study uses the phrase *ontological bifurcation* to describe Radhakrishnan's two-level way of thinking. The position taken here is that by basing his arguments on the results of ontological bifurcation, Radhakrishnan practices dualism. He is a pragmatic dualist. He rejects the Aristotelian law of contradiction when he judges that the choice is not between the reality or unreality of individuals but between the reality or half reality of individuals. However, what does it mean to argue that "a" is either real or half real? Can individuals exist half way? Unless we are willing to set aside the law of contradiction, we cannot explain how there are two levels of reality, neither of which is unreal. There undoubtedly are levels of value, but how can there be levels of fact? Fact "a" either *is* the nature of the case or *is not* the nature of the case. Either individuals exist or they do not exist. Radhakrishnan's pragmatic dualism requires his epistemology of "both this and that." It allows him to maintain the primacy of the one while also maintaining the qualified reality of many individuals.

Incidentally, it is disconcerting to see Radhakrishnan's reliance on this pragmatic dualism after wading through all of his arguments against dualism in *The Reign of Religion in Contemporary Philosophy*.

Radhakrishnan interprets *māyā*[5] as an axiological concept, explaining that "When the Hindu thinkers ask us to free ourselves from *māyā*, they are asking us to shake off our bondage to the unreal values which are dominating us." *Māyā*[5] conceals the real values, he contends. Freedom from *māyā*[5] is the ability to penetrate the veil. It is the state of being related to or united with that which is behind the scrim. It is the state of being released from what Radhakrishnan calls *unreal values*. First the negative and then the positive aspect of his achievement will be considered. His phrase *unreal values* is problematical. It has been noted that Radhakrishnan's philosophy is Indian idealism which includes the proposition that an "idea or value is the operative creative force."[9] *Idea*, *ideal*, and *value* are virtually synonymous concepts throughout Radhakrishnan's system. What, then, is an *unreal value*? How can an Indian idealist conceive of a value which is unreal if ideas or values are the operative creative forces? Values may be relative, created, contingent, *etc*. But how can they be unreal? Likewise, Radhakrishnan's implied phrase *real value* would be redundant. A typically Radhakrishnanian proposition such as *Harmony is real* can never get beyond the pale of the tautological.

The positive aspect of Radhakrishnan's axiological interpretation of *māyā*[5] is that he directs the attention of his Hindu colleagues toward this-worldly values. He presents extensive arguments against Schweitzer's criticism that Hinduism is life- and world-denying. Radhakrishnan conceives values, ideas, and ideals as operative creative forces which must be let loose in life here and now. Tolerance and concord (*samavāya*) are two such values. Despite the fact that Radhakrishnan is vague about the relation between metaphysical and ethical propositions, his untiring effort to make a central place for ethics in *advaita vedānta* thought deserves commendation in the highest degree. As has been noted, he thinks that philosophy should change the world as well as interpret it. He rejects the illusional doctrine of *māyā* "so as to save the world and give to it a real meaning" (appendix

9. IVL, 15.

V). If his *māyā* hermeneutics becomes standard fare in the ashrams and universities of India, it may give rise to a whole new generation of leaders who will be increasingly inspired to rise up and break the spell of an exhausted religious tradtion, an obsolete philosophical watchword ! They will discover in their own Hindu tradition properly understood the ethical motivation and soteriological confidence for improving physical conditions throughout the land.

VI. Māyā[6] : Community, Need, and Affection

Chapter four noted that Radhakrishnan's interpretation of *māyā*[6] has two aspects. *Māyā*[6a] signifies the one-sided dependence of the effect (the world) on the cause (Brahman). *Māyā*[6b] signifies the maintenance of the integrity of the cause.

Radhakrishnan deserves a positive valuation for presenting an argument that Śaṁkara's rope and snake illustration is not intended to convey the world's illusoriness. In *advaita vedānta* tradition, a distinction is made between *pariṇāma* (transformation) and *vivarta* (appearance). Transformation changes the milk into curds but the rope only appears to be a snake. The appearance of the snake which is really a rope is analogous with the appearance of the world which is really Brahman. Brahman appears to be the world. Brahman emanates or lets loose (cf. *sṛṣṭi*) the world. But this "letting loose" is not a transformation because there is no change of substance. Brahman's integrity is maintained in that Brahman does not change into something else during the cosmogonic process of emanation.

To this point, Radhakrishnan's position is compatible with the traditional *advaita vedānta* position. However, he disavows the traditional position when he contends that an *appearance* is not necessarily an *illusion*. Radhakrishnan sees no reason for identifying all appearances as distorted or abnormal perceptions. His position is correct. For instance, opera lovers eagerly await the appearance of the prima donna. Ballet lovers anxiously anticipate the appearance of the prima ballerina and her partner for their pas de deux. Delegates to a national political convention look forward to the appearance of their presidential nominee when it is time for the acceptance speech. These appearances are not illusions. Perceptions of prima donnas, prima ballerinas and presidential nominees are neither distorted nor abnormal perceptions. Likewise, argues Radhakrishnan, the appearance of Brahman as the world is not an illusion.

Incidentally, the problem of *māyā* is exacerbated when the word *illusion* is used imprecisely. Sometimes it is used when the use of *hallucination* would be more appropriate. An hallucination is *a perception of an object which does not exist in the perceiver's physical environment.* The difference between hallucinations and illusions is that hallucinations are perceptions of objects which *do not exist* in the perceiver's physical environment whereas illusions are perceptions of objects which *do exist.* Greater precision in the use of the words *illusion* and *hallucination* would eliminate a great deal of confusion from discussions of *māyā.*

Argument by analogy is persuasive but not conclusive. Śaṁkara's snake and rope analogy has the power of suggestion but one should refrain from pushing the analogy too far. Neither should one fish for a complete explanation of *māyā* in the elusive waters of a desert puddle. Radhakrishnan's positive achievement in interpreting *māyā*^{6a} and *māyā*^{6b} is his intentional omission of the idea that the phenomenal world is an illusion. He takes the position that the world is an appearance (*vivarta*) and that not all appearances are illusions. He contends that the world appearance can be a source of delusion but that it is neither an illusion nor an hallucination.

The reader's attention is now invited to three negative aspects of Radhakrishnan's interpretation of *māyā*^{6a} and *māyā*^{6b}. In the first place, *māyā*^{6a} as one-sided dependence of the effect (world) on the cause (Brahman) eliminates the possibility of community. Community requires two-sided dependence. Community is a relationship among individuals which is characterized by mutual dependence. Community exists where there is a covenant relationship among the communal members. Christian community exists where there is a new covenant in Christ among the members of the community. Through Christ, God enters into a new covenant with his people. The relationship between Jesus and his disciples is the model for the relationship among individuals in the Christian community. Jesus depended on his disciples to spread the news of liberation and release. His disciples depended on him to refresh their memories of the mighty acts of God. The dependence was mutual and two-way. Unfortunately, Radhakrishnan's concepts of unity and continuity provide no basis for building community. Separate individuals must be granted absolute reality if there is to be an absolutely real community. But Radhakrishnan argues that individuals are only relatively real. Using parallel religious doctrines, Radhakrishnan argues that Ātman and Brahman are one. This alleged oneness is what every Hindu is required to remember at every moment. It is a spiritual oneness which is experienced by individuals as individuals. Individuals strive to eliminate all relationships and to seek their own true identities. Anubhava is overcoming the power of *māyā*[5] and eliminating alleged delusions of individuality. It is the elimination of all communal ties and relationships. In short, the difference between Hinduism and Christianity is the difference between the Hindu seeking an identity in isolation and the Christian seeking a relationship in community.

In the second place, Radhakrishnan's interpretation of *māyā*[6a] as the one-sided dependence of the world on the Absolute could eliminate the possibility that persons are a need of God. Need is a personalized form of dependence. Need is characterized by the relationship among individuals in community. Need can be conceived as that without which a personal relationship does not exist. People who do not need people lack an essential ingredient of what it means to be a human being. Need is a two-way dynamic in interpersonal relations. To need friends is one aspect. But being needed by friends is an equally important aspect. Heschel writes:

> Animals are content when their needs are satisfied; man insists not only on being satisfied but also on being able to satisfy, on *being a need* not only on *having needs*. Personal needs come and go, but one anxiety remains: *Am I needed* ? There is no man who has not been moved by that anxiety.[10]

In Heschel's view, *being a need* gives life its meaning and purpose. That persons are *a need of God* is a central aspect of Heschel's

10. Abraham Joshua Heschel, "The Concept of Man in Jewish Thought," in *The Concept of Man: A Study in Comparative Philosophy*, eds. S. Radhakrishnan and P. T. Raju (London: George Allen and Unwin, 1960), p. 109.

Biblical faith. Judaism and Christianity share a tradition of covenantal relationship between men and women and God. The point here is that Radhakrishnan's interpretation of *māyā*[6a] leaves no room for even the remotest possibility that Brahman may have a need of persons. Radhakrishnan sees no way in which it possibly could be said that Brahman is at all dependent on Īśvara, Hiraṇyagarbha, or Virāṭ. He sees no way in which it possibly could be said that Brahman and persons have any relationship whatsoever. In short, the difference between Hinduism and Christianity is the difference between the Hindu whose goal is to transcend either having needs or being a need and the Christian whose goal is to be a need of God.[11]

In the third place, Radhakrishnan's interpretation of *māyā*[6b] as the maintenance of the integrity of the cause eliminates the possibility of affection in the relationship between God and the world. *Affection* is meant in its broadest sense: "I. *Generally* and *literally*. 1. The action of affecting, acting upon, or influencing; or (when viewed passively) the fact of being affected."[12] Affection requires twoness. Affection is action which involves both that which influences and that which is influenced. Strictly speaking, affection is neither personal nor impersonal; affection is a-personal or trans-personal. Colliding billiard balls affect each other. The effect of their collision is a change of velocity. However, affection in human experience is personal. It is so deeply personal that it is difficult if not impossible to funnel affection into theological and philosophical categories. Nevertheless, the fact of affection in human experience must be allowed to mold and shape categories of analysis. Unfortunately, Radhakrishnan's Absolute is affected by nothing. His position is that Brahman's "letting loose" of the world does not affect the integrity of Brahman. In Radhakrishnan's view, the cosmogonic process in no way affects the cause of the process. Creation, preservation, and destruction of the world do not affect the Absolute, he would contend. The power of self-becoming (creation) belongs to Īśvara. Īśvara needs and depends on Brahman, but

11. *To be a need of God* is a recurring theme in Nikos Kazantzakis, *The Saviors of God : Spiritual Exercises* (New York: Simon and Schuster, 1959).

12. *The Oxford English Dictionary*, 12 vols. (Oxford: The Clarendon Press, 1933), s.v. "affection."

not *vice versa*. Brahman is not affected by Īśvara. Chapter four, section six noted Radhakrishnan's statement: "The doctrine of *māyā* declares that the world is dependent on and derived from the ultimate reality. It has the character of perpetual passing away, while the real is exempt from change." It also noted his references to "the fragility of the universe" and "the mutability of things." In short, the difference between Hinduism and Christianity is the difference between the Hindu's experience, according to which events of the world in no way affect Brahman, and the Christian's experience, according to which the God-world relationship is characterized by affection.

VII. Radhakrishnan's Doctrine of Māyā : A General Estimate

Sarvepalli Radhakrishnan is a Hindu modernist. The question remains: "Is Hindu modernism a good way to go?" Chapter three, section four, entitled "A Modernist's Loyalty to Tradition," puts forward Radhakrishnan's description of Śaṁkara as the definition of a modernist. A modernist is someone who is unwilling to break with the past and yet open to the good influences of the new creeds. A modernist is someone who can stretch the old molds without breaking them. In short, a modernist both respects tradition and claims freedom from it. Since the time of Śaṁkara, some Advaita Vedāntins have insisted on an interpretation of *māyā* which says that the world is an illusion. Illusionism has become a rallying point for Hindu fundamentalists like Prabhu Dutt Shastri. However, research for this study suggests that many Advaita Vedāntins since the time of Śaṁkara have rejected an illusional interpretation of *māyā* and that illusionism is not fundamental to Upaniṣadic philosophy or faith. The modernist approach is the proper approach. It demands that we continually re-examine our respective traditions in order to separate the wheat from the chaff. It demands that we continually explore the implications of novel ideas for our respective, ancient faiths.

Does Radhakrishnan stretch the perimeter of Advaita Vedānta beyond recognition? This study concludes that he does not. Traditionally, Advaita Vedāntins have used the following logic:

Brahman is the sole reality; all else is unreal. However, Radhakrishnan's inclusive, wholist conception of Brahman renders this logic faulty. Radhakrishnan's contention stands to reason that the reality of Brahman conceived as the whole *includes* the reality of the universe. Brahman does not exclude the world's reality. Therefore, Radhakrishnan's Advaita Vedānta is very much in keeping with the Upaniṣadic conception of Brahman. It is an inclusive, wholistic conception. The Biblical conception of deity, however, is neither inclusive nor wholist. Unlike Brahman, the Biblical God is no monistic principle which includes all individuals. God is related to other individuals whose reality does not derive from their status as parts of an alleged whole. Even though God is related to all other individuals, the reality of God does not necessarily include the reality of all individuals. Generally speaking, Radhakrishnan's doctrine of *māyā* is unacceptable because it requires a monistic conception of deity—a conception which is inconsistent with the ultimate reality of the many.

Is Radhakrishnan correct in contending that *māyā* as illusion is not a tenet of original Vedānta ? Research conducted for this study supports his position. Radhakrishnan does not conclude that the doctrine of *māyā* is entirely absent from the original Vedānta. It is absent only in the sense of illusion. The question still remains as to how the illusional interpretation of *māyā* crept into Upaniṣadic faith and tradition. Answering this question would require another complete research project.

Does Radhakrishnan interpret the Upaniṣads correctly ? Making a general estimate of Radhakrishnan's Upaniṣadic hermeneutics would go way beyond the scope of this study. Nevertheless, it can be argued that Radhakrishnan's interpretation of the Upaniṣads is free of some basic errors which are found in Prabhu Dutt Shastri's Upaniṣadic exegesis. Shastri argues incorrectly that the *conception* of *māyā* as illusion is found throughout the Upaniṣads and Bādarāyaṇa's *Brahma Sūtras* even though the word *māyā* rarely occurs. Shastri also makes the preposterous suggestion that we insert the allegedly illusional particle *iva*—as it were—into all Upaniṣadic passages which refer to diversity or multiplicity. Finally, Shastri contends incorrectly that philosophical realism in the Upaniṣads is merely a concession to empirical consciousness. Radhakrishnan's interpretation of the Upaniṣads is certainly more felicitous than Shastri's.

Finally, this evaluation returns to the question of ethics. It is Radhakrishnan's intention to stir Hindu hearts for positive ethical action in the secular world. Certainly his writings contain plenty of passages capable of doing this successfully. It is also his intention to counter the Christian charge that Indian thought is world-negating and life-denying. His achievement in this area is a qualified success. World-negation and life-denial are not integral components of the Upaniṣadic worldview; they are later grafts. However, Radhakrishnan's success in pointing this out is qualified by his own two-level way of thinking. His facile categorization of things as penultimate or ultimate blurs his vision of *māyā* and ethics. Ethical action requires that each human act be viewed as urgent and ultimate. In short, every act is ultimate. No act is penultimate. That is,we cannot stop an act when it is only partially completed. Therefore, it makes little sense to speak of penultimate action. This raises serious questions for Radhakrishnan's own ethical system and its connection with his ontology. While he was not particularly concerned to articulate an ethical system, the questions should be raised nevertheless.

To summarize all that has gone before, *māyā*[1] as inexplicable mystery is an epistemological concept. Radhakrishnan contends that things can be seen from an alleged Supreme Identity which lies behind the terrestrial process. But is it possible to see things from the point of view of deity ? Furthermore, Radhakrishnan bifurcates reality into two ontological levels. He uses these two levels epistemologically. But is it possible to make knowledge claims which are based on trans-human experience ? Furthermore, Radhakrishnan contends that the real is the one whereas this writer contends that the real is plural. To his credit, Radhakrishnan points out that the world is neither a distorted nor an abnormal perception even though it is rife with mysteries—wonderful, awesome, inexplicable processes.

Māyā[2] as the power of self-becoming raises cosmogonic issues. *Power of self-becoming* is Radhakrishnan's translation of *ātmavibhūti*, a Sanskrit compound which means the arising, developing, manifesting, expanding, or appearing of the self. Radhakrishnan supports a theory of emanation whereas this study presupposes a theory of creation. *Māyā*² is what this study calls the principle of upagainstness. What Radhakrishnan calls primal consciousness comes up against itself in the emanation of individual consciousnesses. Yet pluralistic realism needs no separate principle of upagainstness such as *māyā*² because the concept of the many already includes sufficient forces of opposition for bringing the actual out of the potential. However, Radhakrishnan deserves tremendous credit for affirming the world which results from the cosmogonic process. He distinguishes between likenesses and illusions. A sculptor makes likenesses which are not illusions. Similarly, Radhakrishnan contends, Īśvara makes a world which is not an illusion.

*Māyā*³ as duality of consciousness (*puruṣa*) and matter (*prakṛti*) indicates Radhakrishnan's position that the world process is a mixture of *sat* and *asat*, being and non-being, self and not-self, spirit and nature, the divine and primal matter, mental events and material events. His interpretation of *māyā*³ is an attempt to incorporate Sāṁkhya dualism into his own Vedānta non-dualism. The attempt fails because the Sāṁkhya position that both *puruṣa* and *prakṛti* are ultimately real is incompatible with the Vedānta position that consciousness is ultimately real whereas matter is penultimately real.

*Māyā*⁴ as primal matter indicates Radhakrishnan's position that matter is real when it is viewed as a part of the whole. This modernist interpretation gets a high mark because it is a vast improvement over Shastri's fundamentalist interpretation of *māyā*. Shastri insists that Brahman alone is real and that everything else including primal matter is an illusion. Such a fundamentalist interpretation of *māyā* tends to dissipate India's motivation for industrialization because it categorizes industrial products as illusions. On the other hand, Radhakrishnan's modernist interpretation of *māyā* gets a low mark because it does not go far enough in granting to primal matter an independent ontological status.

*Māyā*⁵ as concealment indicates Radhakrishnan's soteriological position. He gets a high mark for separating the issue of the world's ontological status from the issue of the world's axiological status. Forms do not cease to exist when they cease to be attractive. They do not cease to exist when they no longer deceive. They do not cease to exist when they no longer have the power to conceal "something more" which is behind them. Just as scientific knowledge regarding the cause of puddles in the desert does not change their ontological status, integral knowledge regarding the cause of the world (Brahman) does not change the world's ontological status. On the other hand, Radhakrishnan gets a low mark for taking the position that individuality is a delusion.

Radhakrishnan's interpretation of *māyā*[6] deserves a positive valuation because it clarifies the intention of Śaṁkara's rope and snake illustration. Radhakrishnan contends that it illustrates the one-sided dependence of the effect (the world) on the cause (Brahman). He argues that it should not be interpreted as an illustration of an alleged illusoriness of the world. Also, Radhakrishnan points out correctly that appearances are not necessarily illusions. On the other hand, Radhakrishnan's interpretation of *māyā*[6] elicits three negative comments. First, it eliminates the possibility of community because community requires two-sided dependence. Second, it eliminates the possibility that persons are a need of God. Need is a personalized form of dependence and Brahman neither needs nor depends on persons. Third, Radhakrishnan's interpretation of *māyā*[6b] eliminates the possibility of affection in the relationship between the world and God

The conclusion of this study is that Radhakrishnan's *māyā* hermeneutics paves the way for future study by Hindus regarding a metaphysical justification for positive ethical action in the modern, secular world. It is also a qualified success in countering the charge from Christians and others that Hinduism is world-negating and life-denying.

Appendix

I

Radhakrishnan's Summary (1923) of Māyā Theory in the Bhagavadgītā

Source: S. Radhakrishnan, *Indian Philosophy*, 2 vols. (London: George Allen and Unwin, 1923, 1927) 1: 546-547.

"To know the exact place of the *māyā* theory in the *Gītā*, it is necessary to distinguish the different senses in which the word is employed, and the exact bearings of the Gītā on them all. (1) If the supreme reality is unaffected by the events of the world, then the rise of these events becomes an inexplicable mystery. The author of the Gītā does not use the term māyā in this sense, however much it may be implied in his views. The conception of a beginningless, and at the same time unreal, avidyā causing the illusion of the world does not enter the mind of the author. (2) The personal Īśvara is said to combine within himself sat and asat, the immutability of Brahman as well as the mutation of becoming.[1] Māyā is the power which enables him to produce mutable nature. It is śakti, or the energy of Īśvara, or ātmavibhūti, the power of self-becoming. Īśvara and māyā in this sense are mutually dependent and are both beginningless.[2] This power of the supreme is called māyā in the Gītā.[3] (3) Since the Lord is able to produce the universe by means of the two elements of His being, prakṛti and puruṣa, matter and consciousness, they are

1. ix. 19.
2. See Śāṇḍilya Sūtras, ii. 13 and 15.
3. xviii. 61; iv. 6.

said to be māyā (higher and lower [*sic*]) of God.[4] (4) Gradually māyā comes to mean the lower prakṛti, since puruṣa is said to be the seed which the Lord casts into the womb of prakṛti for the generation of the universe. (5) As the manifested world hides the real from the vision of the mortals, it is said to be delusive in its character.[5] The world is not an illusion, though by regarding it as a mere mechanical determination of nature unrelated to God, we fail to perceive its divine essence. It becomes the source of delusion. The divine māyā becomes avidyāmāyā. It is so, however, only for us mortals, shut off from the truth; to God who knows it all and controls it, it is vidyāmāyā. Māyā to man is a source of trouble and misery, since it breeds a bewildering partial consciousness which loses hold of the full reality. God seems to be enveloped in the immense cloak of māyā.[6] (6) Since the world is only an effect of God, who is the cause, and since everywhere the cause is more real than the effect, the world as effect is said to be less real than God the cause. This relative unreality of the world is confirmed by the self-contradictory nature of the process of becoming. There is a struggle of opposites in the world of experience, and the real is above all opposites."[7]

4. iv. 16 [*sic*].

5. vii. 14; vii. 25.

6. Māyā which does not produce avidyā is said to be sāttvikī māyā. When it is polluted it breeds ignorance, or avidyā. Brahman reflected in the former is Isvara, while that reflected in the latter is jiva, or the individual self. This is later Vedānta, see Pañcadaśī, i. 15-17. The Gītā is not aware of this view

7. ii 45; vii. 28.

II

Radhakrishnan's Summary (1927) of Māyā in the Advaita Philosophy

Source: S. Radhakrishnan, *Indian Philosophy*, 2 vols. (London: George Allen and Unwin, 1923, 1927) 2:573-574.

"We may bring together the different significations in which the term māyā is used in the Advaita Philosophy. (1) That the world is not self-explanatory shows its phenomenal character, which is signified by the word māyā. (2) The problem of the relation between Brahman and the world has meaning for us who admit the pure being of Brahman from the intuitive standpoint and demand an explanation of its relation to the world, which we see from the logical standpoint. We can never understand how the ultimate reality is related to the world of plurality, since the two are heterogeneous, and every attempt at explanation is bound to fail. This incomprehensibility is brought out by the term māyā. (3) If Brahman is to be viewed as the cause of the world, it is only in the sense that the world rests on Brahman, while the latter is in no way touched by it, and the world which rests on Brahman is called māyā. (4) The principle assumed to account for the appearance of Brahman as the world is also called māyā. (5) If we confine our attention to the empirical world and employ the dialectic of logic, we get the conception of a perfect personality, Īśvara, who has the power of self-expression. This power or energy is called māyā. (6) This energy of Īśvara becomes transformed into the upādhi, or limitation, the unmanifested matter (avyākṛta prakṛti), from which all existence issues. It is the object through which the supreme subject Īśvara develops the universe."

III

Radhakrishnan's Summary (1948) of Māyā

Source: S. Radhakrishnan, *The Bhagavadgītā*, With an Introductory Essay, Sanskrit Text, English Translation and Notes (New York: Harper and Row, Harper Torchbooks, 1973), pp. 42-43.

"We may here distinguish the different senses in which the word 'māyā' is used and indicate its place in the *Gītā*. (1) If the Supreme Reality is unaffected by the events of the world, then the rise of these events becomes an inexplicable mystery The author of the *Gītā* does not use the term, 'māyā,' in this sense, however much it may be implied in his views. The conception of a beginningless, and at the same time unreal, avidyā causing the appearance of the world, does not enter the mind of the author. (2) The personal Īśvara is said to combine within Himself, sat and asat, the immutability of Brahman as well as the mutation of becoming.[2] Māyā is the power which enables Him to produce mutable nature. It is śakti or the energy of Īśvara, or *ātmavibhūti*, the power of self-becoming. Īśvara and māyā in this sense are mutually dependent and beginning-less.[3] This power of the Supreme is called māyā in the *Gītā*.[4] (3) Since the Lord is able to produce the universe by means of the two elements of His being, prakṛti and puruṣa, matter and consciousness, they are said to be māyā (higher and lower [*sic*] of God.[5] (4) Gradually māyā comes to mean the lower prakṛti, since puruṣa is said to be the seed which the Lord casts into the womb of prakṛti for the generation of the universe. (5) As the manifested world hides the real from the vision of mortals, it is said to be delusive in character.[6] The world is not an illusion, though by regarding it as a mere mechanical determination of nature unrelated to God,

2. IX, 19.
3. See *Sāndilya Sūtra* [*sic*], II, 13 and 15; *Svetāsvatara* Up., IV, 10.
4. XVIII, 61; IV, 6.
5. IV, 16 [*sic*].
6. VII, 25 and 14.

we fail to perceive its Divine essence. It then becomes a source of delusion. The Divine māyā becomes *avidyāmāyā*. It is so, however, only for us mortals, shut off from the truth; to God who knows all and controls it, it is *vidyāmāyā*. God seems to be enveloped in the immense cloak of māyā.[7] (6) Since the world is only an effect of God, who is the cause and since everywhere the cause is more real than the effect, the world as effect is said to be less real than God the cause. This relative unreality of the world is confirmed by the self-contradictory nature of the process of becoming. There is a struggle of opposites in the world of experience, and the real is above all opposites.[8]"

IV

Radhakrishnan's Summary (1952) of Māyā in Śaṁkara's System

Source: S. Radhakrishnan et al., eds., *History of Philosophy Eastern and Western*, 2 vols. (London: George Allen and Unwin, 1952, 1953) 1: 279.

"The word *māyā* is used to denote different meanings in Śaṁkara's system: (1) That the world is not self-explanatory shows its phenomenal character, which is signified by the word *māyā*. (2) The problem of the relation between Brahman and the world has meaning for us who admit the pure being of Brahman from the intuitive standpoint and demand an explanation of its relation to the world, which we see from the logical standpoint. We can never understand how the ultimate reality is related to the world of plurality, since the two are heterogeneous, and every attempt at explanation is bound to fail. This incomprehensibil-

7. māyā which does not produce avidyā is said to be *sattvikī maya*. When it is polluted, it breeds ignorance or avidya. Brahman reflected in the former is Isvara, while that reflected in the latter is jīva, or the invidual self. This is later Vedānta; see *Pancadasi*, I, 15-17· *Gita* is not aware of this view.

8. II, 45; VII, 28; IX, 33.

ity is brought out by the term *māyā.* (3) If Brahman is to be viewed as the cause of the world, it is only in the sense that the world rests on Brahman, while the latter is in no way touched by it, and the world which rests on Brahman is called *māyā.* (4) The principle assumed to account for the appearance of Brahman as the world is also called *māyā.* (5) If we confine our attention to the empirical world and employ the dialectic of logic, we get the conception of a perfect personality (Īśvara) who has the power of self-expression. This power or energy is called *māyā.* (6) This energy of Īśvara becomes transformed into the *upādhi,* or limitation, the unmanifested matter (*avyakta prakṛti*) from which all existence issues. It is the object through which the supreme subject Īśvara develops the universe."

V

Radhakrishnan's Summary (1952) of the Status of the World and the Doctrine of Māyā

Source: S. Radhakrishnan, "Reply to Critics," in *The Philosophy of Sarvepalli Radhakrishnan,* ed. Paul Arthur Schilpp (New York: Tudor Publishing Company, 1952), pp. 800-802.

"*The status of the World and the Doctrine of Māyā.* In my writings I have interpreted the doctrine of māyā so as to save the world and give to it a real meaning.

I. (i) The world is derived being. It is an expression of the Absolute and not the Absolute itself. To mark the distinction between Absolute Being and dependent being, we call the latter māyā. When the Absolute is taken as pure being, its relation to the world is inexplicable, *anirvacanīya.* We know that without the background of being there can be no world. The relation between the two cannot be logically explicated. This inexplicability of the logical relationship does not repudiate the existence of the world. It does not say that the world is not, though it appears to be.

To bring out that the changes of the world do not affect the nature of the Absolute, to indicate that the relationship is not one of organic inter-dependence, a distinction is made between *pariṇāma* or modification and *vivarta* or appearance. The one-sided dependence of the world on the Absolute is illustrated by the similes of the appearance of snake in the rope and of silver in the shell. The purpose of these analogies is not to suggest that the world is a dream or an illusion, but that the relationship is such that the world exists without any change in the being of the Absolute.

The world is not a modification of Absolute Being; for in that case Absolute Being would cease to be Absolute and become subject to modifications. We cannot say that a part of the Absolute is modified, whereas the remainder is intact. The Absolute is incapable of being divided into parts.

(ii) Although the Absolute is Eternal Being, the world is temporal being with limits to its existence. A time will come when it will be no more as a process. This essential temporality is indicated by the word *māyā*. This does not make the world into an illusion. To treat it as transitory is not to equate it with the non-existent or the illusory.

II. (i) When the Supreme is viewed not merely as Absolute Being but as Eternal Creativity, the creative power is called māyā. In my account I distinguished Divine Being and Divine action, Absolute in itself, in repose, and the Absolute as active or energising, Brahman and Īśvara. The latter is said to be possessed of *māyā* or power of manifestation. It delights in manifesting.

(ii) As to why this specific possibility was chosen and not any other, one can only say that it is the free act of the Divine. Why did he choose this ? is a question we cannot raise, for the simple reason that God is freedom. By calling creation a mystery, we mean no more than that it is an expression of his freedom, the mysterious working of his will, which is also called *māyā*.

III. In the world process itself, we have the divine interacting with primal matter, what Indian thinkers call the unmanifested *prakṛti*. This is also called *māyā*. The same duality is indicated in the passage of Genesis relating to the Spirit 'moving on the face of the waters.'[8] When the spirit of God brooded on the face of the waters, the original chaos was being shaped into order. As the

8. Genesis, I, 1/2.

dualities between the Divine and the matter, which is used as a means for the unfoldment of the Divine, are not ultimately two separate entities, māyā is not dissociated from the World Spirit. St. John's Gospel refers to light and darkness whose antagonism continues from the initial creation to the final consummation of the world. Two factors, the unbroken energy of light and darkness are affirmed. 'And the light shineth in darkness and the darkness comprehended it not.'[9] All things in the world participate in the characters of this duality. They are *sad-asad-ātmaka*. They are real as well as unreal. This dual character is sometimes indicated by the word *māyā*. The world and the World Spirit are both equally real.

IV. *Māyā* is also used for ignorance by which we do not recognise the principle of the universe. 'He was in the world and the world was made by him and the world knew him not.' This non-knowing is *avidyā*. It is also different from the real and the unreal. If it attains either reality or collapses into nothingness there would be no tension, no process. So the world is said to be *sad-asad-vilakṣaṇa*, different from real and unreal."

9. John I, 4.

Selected Bibliography

Works by Radhakrishnan : Books

Radhakrishnan, Sarvepalli. *The Creative Life*. New Delhi: Orient Paperbacks, 1975.

———. *East and West in Religion*. London: George Allen and Unwin, 1933.

———. *East and West: Some Reflections*. Beatty Memorial Lectures, series no. 1. New York: Harper, 1956; London: George Allen and Unwin, 1956.

———. *Eastern Religions and Western Thought*. Oxford: Clarendon Press, 1939; Oxford University Press paperback, 1969.

———. *Education, Politics and War*. Poona: International Book Service, 1944.

———. *Fellowship of the Spirit*. Cambridge: Harvard University Press, 1961.

———. *Freedom and Culture*. Madras: G. A. Natesan, 1936.

———. *Gautama the Buddha*. Bombay: Hind Kitabs, 1949.

———. *Great Indians*. Introductory essay on the author by Professor D. S. Sarma. Bombay: Hind Kitabs, 1949.

———. *The Heart of Hindusthan*. Madras: G. A. Natesan, 1936.

———. *The Hindu View of Life*. London: George Allen and Unwin, 1927; New York: Macmillan, 1927; Macmillan paperback, 1968.

———. *An Idealist View of Life*. London: George Allen and Unwin, 1932.

———. *India and China: Lectures delivered in China in May 1944*. Bombay: Hind Kitabs, 1944; 3d ed., 1954.

———. *Indian Philosophy*. 2 vols. The Muirhead Library of Philosophy. London: George Allen and Unwin, 1923, 1927; 2d ed., 1929.

———. *Indian Religions*. New Delhi: Vision Books, 1979.

———. *Is This Peace*? Bombay: Hind Kitabs, 1945.

———. *Kalki, Or the Future of Civilization*. London: Kegan Paul, 1929; Ludhiana; Kalyani paperback, 1973.

———. *Occasional Speeches and Writings: October* 1952—*February* 1959. Delhi: Publications Division, Ministry of Information and Broadcasting, Government of India, 1960.

———. *On Nehru*. Delhi: Publications Division, Ministry of Information and Broadcasting, Government of India, 1965.

———. *Our Heritage*. Delhi: Hind Pocket Books, 1973; an Orient paperback.

———. *The Philosophy of Rabindranath Tagore*. London: Macmillan, 1918; also published in Baroda, India: Good Companions, 1961.

———. *The Present Crisis of Faith*. Delhi: Hind Pocket Books, 1970; an Orient paperback.

———. *President Radhakrishnan's Speeches and Writings : Second Series* (*May* 1964—*May* 1967). New Delhi : Publications Division, Ministry of Information and Broadcasting, Government of India, 1969.

———. *Recovery of Faith*. World Perspectives Series, vol. 4. New York: Harper, 1955; London: George Allen and Unwin, 1956.

———. *The Reign of Religion in Contemporary Philosophy*. London : Macmillan, 1920.

———. *Religion and Culture*. Delhi: Hind Pocket Books, 1968; an Orient paperback.

———. *Religion and Society*. 2d ed. London: George Allen and Unwin, 1948.

———. *Religion in a Changing World*. London: George Allen and Unwin, 1967; New York: Humanities Press, 1967; paperback edition.

———. *The Religion We Need*. A Booklet in the Affirmation Series. London: Ernest Benn, 1928.

————. *The Revolutionary Bhoodan Yagna : A Collection of Speeches by S. Radhakrishnan and Others*. Bhoodan Series. Tanjore: Sarvodaya Prachuralaya, 1955.

————. *Sarvepalli Radhakrishnan : vier Ansprachen anlässlich der Verleihung des Friedenspreises des deutschen Buchhandels*. Frankfurt a. M. : Borsenverein des deutschen Buchhandels, 1961.

————. *Two Addresses delivered in Germany, October* 1961. Introductory letter by Theodor Heuss. New Delhi: Max Mueller Bhavan, 1961.

————. *The World's Unborn Soul*. Oxford: Clarendon Press, 1936.

Works by Radhakrishnan : Articles

Radhakrishnan, S. "The Doctrine of Māyā : Some Problems." In *Proceedings of the Sixth International Congress of Philosophy*, pp. 683-689. Edited by E. S. Brightman. New York: Longmans, Green, 1927.

————. *Encyclopedia Britannica*, 14th ed. S.v. "Indian Philosophy," by S. Radhakrishnan.

————. "The Ethics of the Bhagavadgītā and Kant." *International Journal of Ethics* 21 (July 1911): 465-475.

————. "Hinduism and the West." In *Modern India and the West*, pp. 338-353. Edited by L. S. S. O'Malley. Oxford: Oxford University Press, 1941.

————. "My Search for Truth." In *Religion in Transition*, pp. 11-59. Edited by Vergilius Ture Anselem Ferm. New York: Macmillan, 1937. Reprinted in *Radhakrishnan: Selected Writings on Philosophy, Religion, and Culture*, pp. 35-65. Edited by Robert A. McDermott. New York: E. P. Dutton, 1970; a Dutton paperback original.

————. "Religion and Life." *International Journal of Ethics* 27 (October 1916): 91-106.

————. "The Religion of the Spirit and the World's Need: Fragments of a Confession." In *The Philosophy of Sarvepalli Radhakrishnan*, pp. 5-82. Edited by Paul Arthur Schilpp. New York: Tudor, 1952.

————. "Reply to Critics." In *The Philosophy of Sarvepalli Radhakrishnan*, pp. 789-842. Edited by Paul Arthur Schilpp. New York: Tudor, 1952.

————. "The Role of Philosophy in the History of Civilization." In *Proceedings of the Sixth International Congress of Philosophy*. Edited by E. S. Brightman. New York: Longmans, Green, 1927.

————. "UNESCO and World Revolution." *The New Republic* 10 July 1950, pp. 15-16.

————. "The Vedānta Philosophy and the Doctrine of *Māyā*." *International Journal of Ethics* 24 (July 1914): 431-451.

Works Translated by Radhakrishnan

Radhakrishnan, S., trans. and ed. *The Bhagavadgītā*. With an Introductory Essay, Sanskrit Text, English Translation and Notes. London: George Allen and Unwin, 1948; New York: Harper and Row, Harper Torchbooks, 1973.

————. trans. and ed. *The Brahma Sūtra : The Philosophy of Spiritual Life*. With Introductory Essay, Text, Translation, and Notes. New York: Harper, 1960.

————. trans. and ed. *The Dhammapada*. With Introductory Essays, Pāli Text, English Translation and Notes. London: Oxford University Press, 1950; reprinted in Madras by Oxford University Press, 1966.

————. trans. and ed. *The Principal Upaniṣads*. With Introduction, Text, Translation and Notes. London: George Allen and Unwin, 1953; paperback edition, 1968.

Works Edited by Radhakrishnan

Radhakrishnan, S., ed. *Basanta Kumar Mallik: A Garland of Homage from Some Who Knew Him Well*. London: V. Stuart, 1961.

————. and Raju, P. T., eds. *The Concept of Man: A Study in Comparative Philosophy*. London: George Allen and Unwin, 1960; Lincoln, Nebraska: Johnsen, 1960; 2d ed., enl., 1966.

———. and Muirhead, J. H., eds. *Contemporary Indian Philosophy*. The Muirhead Library of Philosophy. London: George Allen and Unwin, 1936; rev. 2d and enl. ed., 1952.

———. et al., eds. *History of Philosophy, Eastern and Western*. 2 vols. London: George Allen and Unwin, 1952, 1953.

———. ed. *Mahatma Gandhi: Essays and Reflections on his Life and Work*. London: George Allen and Unwin, 1939; 2d ed., enl. with a Memorial Section, 1949; Bombay: Jaico, 1957; paperback edition, 1964.

————. Diwakar, R. R., and Swaminathan, K., eds. *Mahatma Gandhi—100 Years*. New Delhi: Gandhi Peace Foundation, 1968.

———. and Moore, Charles A., eds. *A Source Book in Indian Philosophy*. Princeton: Princeton University Press, 1957; paperback edition, 1967.

———. et al., eds. *Wadia, A. R. : Essays in Philosophy Presented in His Honour*. Bangalore: N. A. Nikam, 1954.

Works on Radhakrishnan, with Bibliographies

Arapura, John Geeverghese. *Radhakrishnan and Integral Experience: The Philosophy and World Vision of Sarvepalli Radhakrishnan*. Bombay: Asia Publishing House, 1966.

Bürkle, Horst. *Dialog mit dem Osten: Radhakrishnan's neuhinduistische Botschaft im Lichte christlicher Weltsendung*. Stuttgart: Evangelisches Verlagswerk, 1965.

Cremer, Wilhelm. *Die universale Religion des Geistes: Religion und Religionen bei Sarvepalli Radhakrishnan*. Munich: 1966.

Dutt, Iswara Kunduri, gen. ed. *Sarvepalli Radhakrishnan: A Study of the President of India*. New Delhi: Popular Book Services, 1966.

Harris, Ishwar Chandra. "An Exposition of the Concept of Universalism in Sarvepalli Radhakrishnan's Thought." Ph.D. dissertation, Claremont Graduate School, 1974.

Inge, W. R., Jacks, L. P., Hiriyanna, M., Burtt, E.A., and Raju, P. T., eds. *Radhakrishnan: Comparative Studies in Philosophy Presented in Honour of his Sixtieth Birthday*. New York: Harper, 1948; London: George Allen and Unwin, 1951.

Joad, Cyril Edwin Mitchinson. *Counter Attack from the East: The Philosophy of Radhakrishnan*. London: George Allen and Unwin, 1933.

Matthew, Karimpanamannil Chacko. "Radhakrishnan's and Brunner's Anthropologies: A Comparison." Ph.D. dissertation, Hartford Seminary Foundation, 1956.

McDermott, Robert A. "Radhakrishnan's Comparative Philosophy." Ph.D. dissertation, Boston University, 1969; Ann Arbor, Michigan: University Microfilms, *70-4679.

McDermott, Robert A., ed. *Radhakrishnan: Selected Writings on Philosophy, Religion and Culture*. New York: E. P. Dutton, 1970; a Dutton paperback original.

Michael, Aloysius. *Radhakrishnan on Hindu Moral Life and Action*. Delhi: Concept Publishing Company, 1979.

Nagaraja Rao, P., Gopalaswami, K., and Ramakrishnan, S., eds. *Radhakrishnan Reader : An Anthology*. Selections from the world-famous philosopher-statesman's 40 and odd books written over a period of 60 years. Bombay: Bharatiya Vidya Bhavan, 1969.

Samartha, Stanley Jedidiah. *Introduction to Radhakrishnan: The Man and his Thought*. New York: Association Press, 1964.

Schilpp, Paul Arthur, ed. *The Philosophy of Sarvepalli Radhakrishnan*. The Library of Living Philosophers. New York: Tudor, 1952. Contains T. R. V. Murti's "Bibliography of the writings of Sarvepalli Radhakrishnan to March 1952," pp. 841-861.

Singh, Christ Kumar Paul. *Die Mystik bei Radhakrishnan und die Offenbarungstheologie*. Berlin: 1966.

Tuck, Donald Richard. "Māyā: Interpretative Principle for an Understanding of the Religious Thought of Śaṁkara and Radhakrishnan." Ph.D. dissertation, The University of Iowa, 1970; Ann Arbor, Michigan: University Microfilms, *71-5839.

Urumpackal, Thomas Paul. *Organized Religion According to Dr. S. Radhakrishnan*. Analecta Gregoriana, vol. 184, Series Facultatis Theologicae: Section B, n. 59. Rome: University Gregoriana Editrice, 1972.

Other Works on Radhakrishnan

Atreya, B. L., et al, eds. *Dr. S. Radhakrishnan Souvenir Volume : Collection of 76 Articles by Scholars of International Fame.* Moradabad: Darshana International, 1964.

Benz, Ernst, *Einführung zu : S. Radhakrishnan, Wissenschaft und Weisheit.* Munich: 1961.

Dyal, Sarab, ed. *Sublime Thoughts of S. Radhakrishnan: Extracts from his Speeches and Writings.* Ambala Cantt. : National Publishing House, 1964.

Kalidas, Vuppuluri, ed. *The Radhakrishnan Number: A Souvenir Volume of Appreciations.* Madras: Vyasa Publications, 1962.

Marlow, A. N., ed. *Radhakrishnan: An Anthology.* London: George Allen and Unwin, 1952.

Mascarenhas, Anthony, *A Critique of Sir S. Radhakrishnan's Basis for Human Fellowship*, Lisbon : 1959.

Moses, David Gnanaprakasam, *Professor Radhakrishnan and a Parliament of Religions.* Madras: Christian Literature Society, 1950.

Naravané, Viswanath S., "Radhakrishnan." In *Modern Indian Thought*, pp. 230-264. New York : Asia Publishing House, 1964.

Philosopher and Statesman: A Review of the Visit of H. E. Dr. Sarvepalli Radhakrishnan, President of the Republic of India, to the United States of America, June 1963. Wilmington, Delaware: IBM World Trade Corporation, 1963.

Ray, Santosh Kumar, *The Political Thought of President Radhakrishnan.* Calcutta: Firma K. L. Mukhopadhyay, 1966.

Saher, P. J., *Eastern Wisdom and Western Thought: A Comparative Study in the Modern Philosophy of Religion.* London: George Allen and Unwin, 1969.

Samartha, Stanley Jedidiah, "The Modern View of History: According to Representative Thinkers." Ph.D. dissertation, Hartford Seminary Foundation, 1958.

Sarma, D. S., "Professor Radhakrishnan." In *Studies in the Renaissance of Hinduism in the Nineteenth and Twentieth Centuries*, pp. 585-634. Benares: Benares Hindu University Press, 1944.

Singh, Jagannath S., ed. *Dr. S. Radhakrishnan.* Allahabad: The

Leader Press, 1953. A commemoration volume of articles by J. Singh and others presented to Dr. S. Radhakrishnan at Nath Niwas, Gautam Nagar, Fatehpur, U. P., India in honor of his sixty-sixth birthday.

Singh, Surjit, *Christology and Personality*. Philadelphia: Westminster Press, 1961. Originally a monograph published in India under the title *Preface to Personality : Christology in relation to Radhakrishnan's Philosophy*. Madras: Christian Literature Society for India, 1952.

Works on Māyā

Chauduri, Anil Kumar Ray, *The Doctrine of Māyā*. Calcutta: Dasgupta, 1950.

Devanandan, Paul David, *The Concept of Māyā: An Essay in Historical Survey of the Hindu Theory of the World, with Special Reference to the Vedānta*. London: Lutterworth Press, 1950.

Nagaraja Rao, P., "The Concept of *Māyā* in Advaita." *The Vedānta Kesari* 55 (September 1968).

O'Neil, L. Thomas, *Māyā in Śaṅkara: Measuring the Immeasurable*. Columbia, Missouri : South Asia Books; New Delhi: Motilal Banarsidass, 1980.

Ramakrishna Rao, K. B., *Ontology of Advaita, with Special Reference to Māyā*. Mulki: Vijaya College, 1964.

Ramakrishnan, S. O., "The Doctrine of Māyā." *The Vedānta Kesari* 49 (June 1962): 108-112.

Reddi, Madhusudan, "*Māyā* and *Māyāvāda* : A Critical Retrospect." *The Vedānta Kesari* 51 (September 1964): 103-106.

Reyna, Ruth, *The Concept of Māyā: From the Vedas to the 20th Century*. Bombay: Asia Publishing House, 1962.

Shastri, Prabhu Dutt, *The Doctrine of Māyā in The Philosophy of the Vedānta*. London: Luzac, 1911.

Other Works

Bhattacharya, Harisatya, *Anekantavada*. Bhavnagar: Shri Jain Atmanand Sabha, 1953.

Bosch, F. D. K., *The Golden Germ: An Introduction to Indian Symbolism.* The Hague, Netherlands: Mouton, 1960.

Bradley, F. H., *Appearance and Reality.* 2d ed. Oxford: Clarendon Press, 1897; Oxford University Press paperback, 1969.

Bruteau, Beatrice, "The Reality and Value of the World in the Philosophy of Sri Aurobindo." Ph.D. dissertation, Fordham University, 1969.

Burlingame, Eugene Watson, "The Act of Truth (Saccakiriya): A Hindu Spell and its Employment as a Psychic Motif in Hindu Fiction." *Journal of the Royal Asiatic Society* (1917): 429-467.

Heschel, Abraham Joshua. "The Concept of Man in Jewish Thought." In *The Concept of Man: A Study in Comparative Philosophy,* pp. 108-157. Edited by S. Radhakrishnan and P. T. Raju. London: George Allen and Unwin, 1960; Lincoln, Nebraska: Johnsen, 1960.

Hutchison, John Alexander, *Paths of Faith.* New York: McGraw-Hill, 1969; 3rd ed., 1981.

————, "Theology in Global Context." In *Philosophy of Religion and Theology* : 1971. Edited by David Griffin. Chambersburg, Pennsylvania: American Academy of Religion, 1971.

Lanman, Charles Rockwell, *A Sanskrit Reader.* Text and Vocabulary and Notes. Cambridge: Harvard University Press, 1920: reprinted, 1967.

Monier-Williams, Monier, *A Sanskrit-English Dictionary.* New edition, greatly enlarged and improved. Oxford: Clarendon Press, 1899; reprinted, 1964. Motilal Banarsidass, Delhi, 1984.

Moore, Charles A., "Metaphysics and Ethics in Radhakrishnan's Philosophy." In *The Philosophy of Sarvepalli Radhakrishnan,* pp. 279-312. Edited by Paul Arthur Schilpp. New York: Tudor, 1952.

Muirhead, J. H., "The Hindu Idea of Truth." In *Mahatma Gandhi: Essays and Reflections on his Life and Work.* Edited by S. Radhakrishnan. London: George Allen and Unwin, 1939.

Nakamura, Hajime, *Ways of Thinking of Eastern Peoples.* Rev.

English translation. Ed. Philip P. Wiener. Honolulu: East-West Center Press, 1964.

The Oxford English Dictionary. 12 vols. Oxford: Clarendon Press, 1933.

A corrected re-issue with an Introduction, Supplement, and Bibliography of *A New English Dictionary* on historical principles founded mainly on the materials collected by The Philological Society and edited by James A. H. Murray, Henry Bradley, W. A. Craigie, and C. T. Onions.

Potter, Karl H., *Presuppositions of India's Philosophies*. Englewood Cliffs, New Jersey: Prentice-Hall, 1963.

Sinari, Ramakant A., *The Structure of Indian Thought*. A monograph in The Bannerstone Division of American Lectures in Philosophy. Springfield, Illinois : Charles C. Thomas, 1970.

Smith, Wilfred Cantwell, "Comparative Religion: Whither—and Why?" In *The History of Religions*: *Essays in Methodology*, pp. 31-58. Edited by Mircea Eliade and Joseph M. Kitagawa. Chicago: University of Chicago, Phoenix Book, 1959.

————, *The Meaning and End of Religion*. New York: New American Library, Mentor Book, 1962.

Whitney, William Dwight, *The Roots, Verb-Forms, and Primary Derivatives of the Sanskrit Language*. Leipzig: Breitkopf and Härtel, 1885: New Haven, Connecticut: American Oriental Society, 1945. (Rept.) 1975, Motilal Banarsidass, Delhi.

Wolff, Otto, *Radhakrishnan*. Göttingen : 1962.

Zaehner, Robert Charles, trans. and ed. *The Bhagavadgitā*. With a Commentary and Transliteration of original Sanskrit. Oxford: Clarendon Press, 1969; Oxford University Press Paperback, 1973.

Zimmer, Heinrich, *Philosophies of India*. Princeton : Princeton University Press, 1951.

Index